Reading Visual Investigations

Reading Visual Investigations

Between Advocacy, Journalism, and Law
Edited by Lisa Luksch and Andres Lepik

06	**Examine, Interpret, Present** Lisa Luksch and Andres Lepik
14	**The Impact of Visual Data on Human Rights Advocacy** Sam Dubberley in Conversation with Andres Lepik
26	CASE STUDY **US Policing and the Suppression of Dissent**
32	CASE STUDY **A City within a Building:** **The Russian Air Strike on Mariupol's Theater**
38	**How Open Source Intelligence Improves Investigative Journalism** Lea Weinmann
46	**Not Fit for Purpose?** **Climate Law, Science, Technology, and the People on the Frontlines** Anjli Parrin
60	CASE STUDY **What Is Owed?** **Taking the Climate Crisis to the World Court**
68	**Empowering Critical Literacy** Laura Kurgan in Conversation with Andres Lepik
82	CASE STUDY **Investigating Xinjiang's Network of Detention Camps**

92 **The Violent Image, Tunnel Vision, and Blind Faith: Reflections on the Argumentative Potency of Visual Investigations**
Bora Erden

104 CASE STUDY

In Plain Sight: Remote Sensing and Land Dispossession in the West Bank

114 **3D Crime Scenes: Forensic Reconstruction and Visualization**
Ralf Breker

128 CASE STUDY

The Sound of Bullets: Investigating the Killing of Colombian Journalist Abelardo Liz

134 CASE STUDY

Documenting the Death Flights

140 **Initiating the Counter Evidentiary Network: Toward a "Solidarity-Based" Mode of Open Source Investigation**
Patrick Brian Smith

148 **Fortifying the Truth**
Sam Gregory in Conversation with Lisa Luksch

Examine, Interpret, Present

Lisa Luksch and Andres Lepik

The Universal Declaration of Human Rights, adopted by the United Nations in 1948, was a significant step toward establishing an ethical compass for globalization. Since then, violations of these rights are no longer purely national matters, but affect us all and can be prosecuted in international courts. But how do we ensure that these rights are actually protected and enforced in an increasingly interconnected and complex world? This is precisely where the field of visual investigations comes in—a field that is dedicated to the image-based investigation of human rights violations and is thus breaking new ground in promoting justice and accountability. *Visual Investigations: Between Advocacy, Journalism, and Law* arose from our belief that architecture plays a central role in this endeavor. Architecture can not only shape, but also help strengthen the mechanisms of advocacy and accountability. With this reader, we would like to make the current discourse on visual investigations accessible and show how architectural expertise actively contributes to uncovering human rights violations and making them visible.

Wherever there are humans, says Sam Dubberley in an interview, there is always architecture. And therefore, wherever human rights violations take place, the reconstruction of space and environment is helpful in clarifying them. Dubberley, the head of digital investigations at Human Rights Watch, explains why for around fifteen years now more and more architects have been involved in uncovering human rights violations around the world. Such violations are more present than ever before, not least of all due to the ubiquitous availability of image sources in public discourse: smartphones, satellites, and surveillance and police cameras document injustice and violence all over the world, even in places where we are denied physical access and personal reporting. The linking of this video and image content with people, places, and events has thus been established for some time now as a new field for architecture in close cooperation with other disciplines and has led to momentous findings and even court rulings at an international level.

The exhibition *Visual Investigations: Between Advocacy, Journalism, and Law* and the accompanying reader are the result of an interdisciplinary exchange between the Architecture Museum of the Technical University of Munich (TUM), four internationally active research teams and their respective cooperation partners, and a number of experts from academic and professional contexts. Our use of the term "visual investigations" is based on the name of the corresponding investigative department of *The New York Times,* which was founded in 2017. Driven by the question of the role of the architectural profession and of architects themselves in uncovering and visualizing human rights violations, we initiated a number of conversations in the summer of 2023. We contacted the architect Alison Killing, whose installation on the network of detention camps in Xinjiang at the Venice Architecture Biennale in 2023 was profoundly disturbing. Through Killing (who has since become a senior reporter for the visual investigations team of the *Financial Times*) and her network, we came into contact with Bellingcat, an international research collective based in Amsterdam that became especially well known for their investigation of the crash of the MH17 flight over eastern Ukraine. At the same time, we spoke to Brad Samuels, co-founder of SITU Research in New York City, one of the leading organizations in the field, whose educational work focuses on injustices in the context of human rights, the environment, and police work.

Through collaboration with the Center for Spatial Technologies (CST), a research network operating from Kyiv and Berlin at the interface of architecture, social sciences, and art, the exhibition also features an investigation carried out jointly with Forensic Architecture (FA), a research agency founded in 2010 by Eyal Weizman at the Centre for Research Architecture at Goldsmiths, University of London. Forensic Architecture has long shaped the field of the same name; it has already been shown in numerous exhibitions, particularly in Germany, and has become well known there, not least of all for its research into the NSU complex. However, Eyal Weizman has cancelled Forensic Architecture's participation in our group exhibition.

Our aim with *Visual Investigations* is to present a comprehensive exhibition that offers different perspectives, methods, and approaches and makes visible various collaborations and protagonists from the linked areas of advocacy, journalism, and law. The exhibition reader presents seven case studies on five continents in texts that examine the backgrounds, methods, content, and consequences of the research. Each of the projects in the exhibition is accompanied by visual material, including archive footage, satellite images, 3D models, and video stills. Readers of the book also have opportunity to access selected visual material by scanning QR codes in order to see exhibition views, updates on ongoing investigations, and even entire film clips. The content behind these QR codes is stored not on web servers or in the cloud, but rather on a blockchain basis in order to forestall attacks on or manipulation of the data and guarantee security of access. These measures prevent the results of investigations—which are often deemed undesirable by those responsible for the human rights violations—from being distorted or the content being taken down by third parties. The contributions include research into land dispossession in occupied territories and the consequences of the climate crisis for residents of Pacific Island states, where violence is only implicitly recognizable. But in other cases, viewers also encounter explicit descriptions and visualizations of violence, to which we would like to alert our readers in advance.

In addition to the content of the exhibition, this book presents eight texts that underline the interdisciplinarity of the field. The authors and topics range from Laura Kurgan, who can be considered one of the founders of the discipline with her Spatial Information Design Lab established in 2004 and who tells us about critical data visualization at Columbia University, to Ralf Breker's work on 3D crime scenes at the Bavarian State Office of Criminal Investigation, to the founding of a network for counter-evidence by Patrick Brian Smith, which a large number of visual investigators around the world have already joined. Two journalistic contributions show how differently the German and US media view the current status of visual investigations: Lea Weinmann writes about the possibilities of open source intelligence (OSINT), which the *Süddeutsche Zeitung* has been using since Russian soldiers invaded Ukraine in 2022, while

Bora Erden, a member of the visual investigations team of *The New York Times,* points out the limitations of the new practice.

In a world in which political and military conflicts as well as the consequences of climate change are forcing more and more people to flee and protest, it seems logical that architecture is also increasingly taking on the task of exposing violence and injustice. In close cooperation with other disciplines, architecture can use its complex tools to stand up for humanity and ethical values, from spatial analysis and 3D modeling to artificial intelligence and machine learning. The aim should always be to show and present facts and connections in a manner that is as factual, transparent, objective, and independent as possible. Against the current backdrop of global competition for the right to interpret politically controversial events and the acute threat to finding truth and enlightenment through targeted misinformation, visual investigations is developing rapidly as a discipline and can actively contribute to highlighting and prosecuting the violations of human rights condemned by the global community.

Scan the QR code to
see exhibition views
and documentation of
the public program.

NYPD's body-worn camera captures police violence during a Black Lives Matter demonstration in the Bronx neighborhood of Mott Haven.

The Impact of Visual Data on Human Rights Advocacy

Sam Dubberley [SD] in Conversation with Andres Lepik [AL]

SAM DUBBERLEY

Sam Dubberley is the director of the Technology, Rights & Investigations division at Human Rights Watch (HRW), leading the organization's work on the use of technology to investigate human rights violations and the risks technology poses to our human rights. He is also a fellow of the Human Rights Centre at the University of Essex and coeditor of the book *Digital Witness: Using Open Source Information for Human Rights Investigation, Documentation, and Accountability,* published by Oxford University Press. He has published widely on the impact of viewing harmful content during open source investigation and the risk of vicarious trauma.

ANDRES LEPIK

Andres Lepik is the director of the Architecture Museum at the Technical University of Munich and a professor of architectural history and curatorial practice there. After studying art history and completing his dissertation on Renaissance architectural models, he worked as a curator at the Neue Nationalgalerie in Berlin and in the Architecture and Design Department of The Museum of Modern Art, New York.

ANDRES LEPIK   Sam, you work at the interface between technology and human rights. How did this come about and what characterizes your day-to-day work today?

SAM DUBBERLEY   *(laughs)* Sadly, as a director, my day-to-day work is mostly about budgets and human resource issues. But for the sake of this interview, let's pretend I'm still something of a researcher. I've been working at this interface between technology and human rights since the Arab Spring. I think it was an interesting time that allowed us to see the power of mobile phones and remote sensing, of satellite imagery and the possibilities for researching human rights violations, especially in the context of war. In 2010, 2011, before the Arab Spring, we were often reliant on state television—Syrian, Egyptian state television—to receive visual information. And I think the developments in technology—like phone cameras and social media, for example—changed all that. They allow for people to tell their own stories and share experiences of what they have witnessed. And for us as human rights organizations, these shared experiences provide the opportunity to get a better idea of what is going on all over the world, especially in places we cannot access.

In the Digital Investigations Lab at Human Rights Watch, our day-to-day work is really about working on conflicts. Sadly, there are too many conflicts in our world today, and we work on all of them, be it the conflict in Gaza, Sudan, Myanmar, or Ethiopia. We keep looking at all of those places. And we use satellite imagery, videos and photographs, flight tracking data, and more to then compare the findings with the interviews we do. It is still crucial for us to speak to people, victims of violations, and to understand what they have experienced. But we do now use technology to back it up. A lot of the work we do is about finding information and then verifying it. In a world where facts are so contested, it is important that Human Rights Watch is perceived as an objective voice that can help establish facts.

AL   Could you elaborate a bit more on the advantages of working with digital evidence for HRW's practice?

SD   I think for us it is a variety of things. There is a lot of persuasive power in digital evidence. Human Rights Watch exists not only to report, but also to make change happen, and digital research really has the power to change opinions, to make people understand situations in parts of the world they might not know about. And this, in turn, has an impact on people in positions of power. In order to make change happen, we speak to people in those positions, whether in Berlin or Addis Ababa, Tokyo, Washington, DC, or São Paolo—basically in any major decision-making part of the world.

Secondly, the work our Digital Investigations Lab is doing allows us to access places that would otherwise be inaccessible. The world that we as HRW can access is getting smaller. Once upon a time, we could travel to Hong Kong without any problems. Now we can no longer travel there; we cannot travel to Iran. Nowadays, there are lots of places in the world we just can't access. But thanks to digital investigations, we can still see what is going on there. And I think that is a real advantage of working with digital evidence: it makes the world of people who commit human rights abuses, who violate the laws of war, smaller. It means that they cannot hide, it means that we can see what they are trying to hide. That is one of the biggest advantages.

AL   Referring to our exhibition and the emerging interest of architecture in the investigation and visualization of human rights violations: What role does the visual processing of data play for HRW? Can you tell us about past cooperation with research networks and architects?

SD   We have done several collaborations, in particular with SITU Research, an architectural practice focused on visual investigations. A few years ago we developed a piece together with SITU that sheds light on the disproportionate use of police force during protest marches in Mott Haven in the Bronx, USA. → CASE STUDY, PAGES 26–31

AL   This investigation is part of our exhibition, too.

SD   That's fantastic! It's a great example to show the impact of visual processing of data: in an incident like this, everybody is out there with their phones and cameras, documenting what is going on and sharing it on social media. If all this information is gathered, it creates a pretty damning picture. Yet with each individual fragment of information, it is difficult to get that full picture, to understand the temporal and spatial sequence of events. Only the analysis and visual processing of this data helps us to understand the anatomy of the situation.

In the Mott Haven piece, going through the material step by step, understanding what fits where in the time chain and on the map, allowed us to prove the police's intention to stop people from leaving the protests before the nighttime curfew during the Covid-19 pandemic. People were blocked, encircled, and later arrested.

If you are confronted only with pieces of information, people individually complaining about what they had experienced, it's hard to understand that there was an intention. Whereas if you map it out, it becomes unimpeachable, it becomes irrefutable. The visual argumentation basis we created was enormously powerful.

We have done similar things in other locations as well. We used video analysis in an investigation in Myanmar where protesters were also "kettled" and in this case killed. We have worked on the Russian invasion of Ukraine to show the spatial extent of the destruction of Mariupol. Again in collaboration with SITU Research, we wanted to systematically document the damage over a three-month period. We had to go through each individual piece of

18   Sam Dubberley in Conversation with Andres Lepik

visual evidence on its own, from phone camera to surveillance footage, drone data, and more, and find out where and when exactly it was captured. In the end, we found out that about 93% of apartment buildings in Mariupol were damaged to some extent. And I know what you might think: do we really need to do this in such detail? But the impact this has on justice, accountability, and collective memory is truly significant. In a world where facts are contested, visual evidence and its accurate labeling and processing make it much harder to refute them.

AL Visual investigations is an interdisciplinary field that not only consists of a variety of professions but also contributes to various other professional fields and their own logics. How does your work in advocacy differ from your work in court cases? Is there a difference in the approach?

SD There is a difference. It is important to note that Human Rights Watch is not a prosecutorial organization. We are an advocacy organization; and our goal is to make change happen. We are trying to persuade decision-makers to make a difference. And bringing visual information into advocacy makes people care, makes people listen, makes them stand up.

Last year, we did some research into killings at the Saudi Arabia–Yemen border. Saudi border guards were killing hundreds of migrants, mostly from Ethiopia, who tried to cross the border from Yemen to Saudi Arabia between March 2022 and June 2023. That was not new information; we did not uncover something amazingly new. Everybody with an interest in that part of the world knew it was happening. The UN and some NGOs had written about it. But we were the first ones to collect all the visual evidence, verify it, and build a 3D topographical model from it. The model made visible that the Saudi border guards were able to identify the people as migrants. They were able to recognize their traditional dress. Despite comprehensive visibility, the guards still killed those people.

Our findings generated a lot of attention. One of the results of our research was that Germany temporarily suspended their training support for the Saudi border guards, and so did the US. Our report ended up on the front page of *The New York Times.*

But will this lead to justice? Will this lead to court proceedings anywhere? Probably not. But we were able to stop the killings, at least for a short while. I do believe that with our advocacy pieces we can achieve immediate change. On top of that, we are thinking a lot about how to support the work of prosecutors, how to make our work available and usable for them to build on. It is not our job to tell the International Court of Justice what to do. It is not our job to tell prosecutors anywhere in the world what to do. But we hope that our research and our information can lead them to new ideas. The research we did on Mariupol, for example, got picked up in a case at the European Court of Human Rights in Strasbourg. I do think that visual information and the work of visual investigators will become more important, not only in our work, but also in court.

AL   That brings me to my next question: How do judicial authorities and legal institutions react to these new forms and instruments of information?

SD   The quality and type of evidence has changed throughout history, and the judiciary has had to adapt to that. Nearly 200 years ago, the first photographs emerged and started to be used in court; not long after that, film emerged and was integrated as well over time. However, the pace of change is the issue. And I think judges need to understand how to analyze information. Judges are experienced at listening to experts, interrogating people, and trying to find out whether what they say is correct. But as more and more visual evidence finds its way into courtrooms, it is not only prosecutors, but also the defense, for example, who has to understand how to deal with this form of information. But I think with time comes change. Just this week [June 26, 2024] the International Criminal Court convicted Mr. Al Hassan Ag Abdoul Aziz Ag Mohamed Ag Mahmoud of war crimes and crimes against humanity committed in Timbuktu, Mali, during 2012 and 2013, based on social media videos and a platform featuring a 3D model of the built environment of Timbuktu by SITU Research. I am convinced that the influence of visual evidence in courts all over the world will grow. But let's not forget that talking to witnesses, talking to victims, will never be replaced by progress in technology.

AL　Which technological developments do you think will have the greatest impact on your work in the coming years, both positively and negatively? What role does AI play in the future of your work?

SD　I believe that in addition to all the risks and challenges that this technology brings, we also need to understand how it can support our work. And as with any other technology, we must approach it through the lens of human rights. In all of our visual investigation work, we must ensure that we ourselves do not abuse people's rights—the right to privacy, for example, or the right to security and safety. The risk of violating these rights is comparatively high when using Artificial Intelligence.

We are confronted with AI-generated videos and photographs, as well as AI-generated audio—so called "deepfakes" of people's voices. Verifying and cross-checking such data is one of our biggest challenges, and can be more complicated in Sudan or Myanmar than verifying something German Chancellor Olaf Scholz is said to have stated. We have to be careful. We have to stick to our proven methodologies, our bread and butter, if you will: speaking to people, learning about their experiences, and seeing if everything lines up. And only then can we start thinking about how AI could support our work. How does it help us find information? How does it help us construct models?

Rather than spending five days constructing them in computer programs like Blender, we can task AI to do it. We can task AI to do calculations. We can save time and therefore act faster.

It is an exciting time, and there is a lot of technology that we as an advocacy organization can profit from as well. One example is augmented reality: Haiti is currently an inaccessible, dangerous place. Few people are interested in what is happening there. But if we can use virtual reality to "bring" people to the streets of Port au Prince, they can better understand the situation there. If we can "take" decision-makers to the Pacific Islands, would they better understand the risk of losing their homes due to climate change? Can technology awaken empathy and understanding for circumstances that otherwise remain abstract and inaccessible?

We tend to focus on the challenges related to AI, but it's exciting to think about the opportunities as well.

AL   Apart from the obvious dangers that human rights investigative research can entail, you also describe the risk of vicarious trauma in one of your latest publications. What risks—perhaps unexpected ones—do research teams expose themselves to and what is your advice?

SD   This work, investigating human rights violations, is hard. I have colleagues who travel around the world to visit the scenes of the most horrific crimes. And they talk to people who witnessed these crimes—people who have lost their homes, their children, their families. It is awful. And it is traumatic. At the same time, my team and I look at videos of this. Not only do we have people's verbal recollections of events, but we have videos documenting what they are left with. Cities reduced to gray rubble.

What I want to make people aware of is that all of these traumas are real, both experiencing it firsthand and sitting in front of your computer, looking at your screen in a Berlin office, for example. We have to take all of these levels of trauma that come with human rights work very seriously. I'm forty-seven years old. I've been working with traumatic imagery since the 9/11 attacks. After more than twenty years, I thought I was "pretty strong," like "I have seen it all." But the last twelve months have been deeply traumatic for me. I thought I had it all built up, had my protective measures ready: meditating, going for a walk in nature, not drinking too much beer, all these sorts of things. Yet still, it can come at you out of nowhere. Over the last year, two years really, since the invasion of Ukraine, I have been affected by it, even though I thought I was okay.

It is a topic I care about a lot, not only personally, but also for my team: I care about it because we want this work to be sustainable. We want people to be able to investigate human rights abuses in the long run, because—let's face it—the world is not going in a good direction and there is not too much optimism out there. Injustice is not going to stop. Human rights abuses are not going to stop. That's why we're trying to build a culture around it. And what I realized is that having a good team around you, where people trust and support each other, is a way to get through and protect yourself from vicarious trauma.

AL   Thank you. If I may, I would like to add the following question at the end: As an architecture museum, we have taken on this topic because we have the feeling that more and more architects are working in this discipline. How do you see the role of architects in this emergent field?

SD   I think that wherever there are humans, there is architecture to some extent. And wherever human rights abuses happen, space and structures and buildings are involved. That involvement can range from the mere location or environment of an event to specific elements of an architecture that can help reconstruct events. Architectural and spatial knowledge can be crucial to understanding and reconstructing. An example could be people who seek shelter underneath a building. What kind of bomb does it require to destroy that building? This is something we saw a lot in Ukraine, and we started to investigate it. There were huge apartment blocks with big holes in the middle and people had been killed on the lower floors. Only one person had survived and an architect helped us understand the structure of the building and why this one person was able to survive.

Architectural knowledge helps us understand how we interact with the physical space that we inhabit, how we perceive space and see things. But architects also provide an understanding of how cities and buildings are constructed, and they are equipped with a specific set of techniques to analyze and visualize; they know about measuring, photogrammetry, software ... all these things are really important for our work, as we want to be as detailed as we can possibly be. I have had an amazing time working with architects. I always learn so much from them, and they do really push us forward when it comes to investigating human rights abuses.

US Policing and the Suppression of Dissent

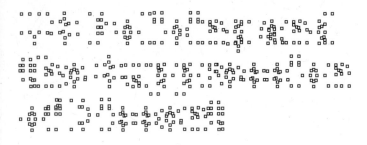

SITU Research, New York City, in collaboration with Human Rights Watch (HRW) and the National Lawyers Guild's BLM/Floyd Litigation Task Force

2020 and 2022–23

SITU RESEARCH

SITU Research is a practice focused on visual investigations, leveraging innovative fact-finding methods to cut through digital noise and amplify truth. Comprising designers, urbanists, computer scientists, and analysts, SITU Research synthesizes various forms of digital evidence to create comprehensive, factual accounts of contested events. Their work addresses issues such as human rights, environmental justice, policing, and civil liberties.

Project participants, 2020: Gauri Bahuguna, Bora Erden, Griffin Frazen, Jon Nealon, Helmuth Rosales, and Brad Samuels; 2022–23: Gauri Bahuguna, Ramón Bieri, Evan Grothjan, Akshay Mehra, Jon Nealon, Brad Samuels, and Candice Strongwater

HUMAN RIGHTS WATCH

Human Rights Watch (HRW) investigates and reports on abuses happening in all corners of the world. It is an international non-governmental organization (NGO) of roughly 550 people of more than seventy nationalities, including country experts, lawyers, and journalists who work to protect the most at risk, from vulnerable minorities and civilians in wartime to refugees and children in need. They direct their advocacy toward governments, armed groups, and businesses, pushing them to change or enforce their laws, policies, and practices.

BLM/FLOYD LITIGATION TASK FORCE

Founded in 1937, the National Lawyers Guild (NLG) is a progressive public interest association of lawyers, law students, paralegals, jailhouse lawyers, law collective members, and other activist legal workers, in the United States. The NLG's BLM/Floyd Litigation Task Force consisted of Wylie Law, Cohen& Green, Beldock Levine & Hoffman, Gideon Orion Oliver, with Rosa Palmeri and Andrew Sawtelle

From late May to early November 2020, thousands of civil rights demonstrators gathered to protest police brutality following the murder of George Floyd, a Black man who was killed by police officers in Minneapolis, Minnesota, on May 25, 2020. In the following weeks, protests demanding an end to police violence took place across the United States. Portland, Chicago, and New York City were among the cities where law enforcement sought to control and, in some cases, suppress these protests.

The investigators explore one of these contexts in detail: New York City. Over the course of several months, the New York Police Department (NYPD) responded with widespread and varied use of force. The irony of marches protesting police brutality, particularly against communities of color, being marred by the excessive application of force was not lost on anyone.

Throughout these marches, the NYPD—increasingly equipped and trained as a paramilitary force in the years since 9/11— assaulted protesters, bystanders, and legal observers with baton strikes to the head and body, tackled them to the ground, and subjected them to excessively tight "zip-tie" handcuffs, pepper spray, and a tactic called "kettling,"[1] often used to trap protesters before making mass arrests. Starting on May 28 and continuing through at least November, nearly 3,500 people were brutally injured or jailed. These incidents, which violated a wide range of constitutional rights such as freedom of speech, press, and assembly, were captured on video in a variety of formats, including protesters documenting events on their phones, body cameras worn by police officers, aerial surveillance imagery, and CCTV footage. Given the deluge of documentation, video became the primary source of evidence used to analyze the NYPD's use of force and to evaluate their response to the protests.

Two investigations by SITU Research emerge from this period of civil unrest and suppression of dissent. The first is the advocacy video *The Trap* from 2020, an event reconstruction produced with Human Rights Watch that focuses on a protest that descended into police-initiated violence in the Bronx

28   Case Study

Police footage was provided to SITU Research by member attorneys from the National Lawyers Guild (NLG) during the period of discovery for the class action lawsuit Sow et al. v. City of New York et al. NYPD police body-worn camera footage (bottom) and NYPD helicopter footage (top) capture protests during the Black Lives Matter movement in 2020.

neighborhood of Mott Haven. The second project, commissioned in 2023 by member attorneys from the National Lawyers Guild, looked at patterns of police violence across over eighty locations in New York City and required sifting through thousands of police body camera recordings, helicopter surveillance footage and smartphone videos captured by protesters. The extensive research consisted of analyzing a vast collection of protest videos to help certify the class action lawsuit *Sow et al. v. City of New York et al.*

In both cases, the unique role of video analysis is evident, exemplifying the visual turn in advocacy and law aimed at holding police and government officials accountable for their actions or misconduct.

The public release of *The Trap* exposed the NYPD's unlawful police tactics and New York's Mayor de Blasio's misrepresentation of what happened that day in the Bronx. The lawsuit *Sow* culminated in an over 13-million-dollar settlement—the largest sum awarded to protesters in the history of the United States—constituting a public referendum on the NYPD's protocols, and methods for dealing with protests.

---

1 Kettling, also referred to as containment or corralling, is a police strategy used to control large crowds during demonstrations or protests. This tactic involves forming extensive cordons of police officers who then work to confine the crowd within a restricted area. Protesters may exit through police-controlled exits, slip through uncontrolled gaps in the cordon, or be contained, thereby preventing them from leaving and leading to their arrest.

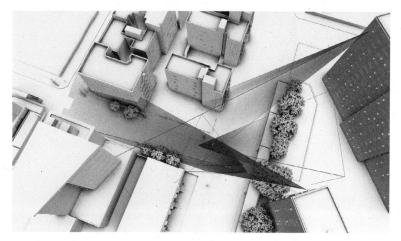

Site model reconstruction showing the cones of view of five simultaneous videos captured during a demonstration in Mott Haven, Bronx.

Codec is a collaborative, digital tool developed by SITU Research for managing, analyzing, and presenting video evidence.

Scan the QR code for additional information and to watch processed video footage of the protests.

US Policing and the Suppression of Dissent

A City within a Building

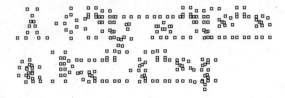

The Russian Air Strike on Mariupol's Theater

The Center for Spatial Technologies (CST), Kyiv and Berlin, in collaboration with Forensic Architecture, London, and Forensis, Berlin

2022–ongoing

THE CENTER FOR SPATIAL TECHNOLOGIES

The Center for Spatial Technologies (CST), founded in 2018, is a transdisciplinary research group based in Kyiv and Berlin at the intersection of architecture, the social sciences, and investigative and artistic practices. Focused on the multifaceted study of urban environments across time, CST collaborates with a diverse array of cultural, academic, and human rights organizations to render visible important societal issues and their spatial implications. CST's works are featured on leading global platforms, including *The New York Times,* the Venice Biennale, and Ukrainian President Volodymyr Zelensky's social media.

Project participants: Maksym Rokmaniko, Mykola Holovko, Daryna Vilkhova, Ksenia Rybak, Valeria Prorizna, Andrii Onyshchenko, Oksana Hrabchak, Sasha Zakrevska, Natasha Pereverzina, Herman Mitish, and Orest Yaremchuk

FORENSIC ARCHITECTURE

Forensic Architecture (FA) is a research agency based at Goldsmiths, University of London. Since 2010, they have coined the term "Forensic Architecture" to refer to the production and presentation of spatial evidence within legal, political, and cultural contexts, taking architecture to include not only buildings but shaped environments at the scale of cities and territories.

Project participants: Eyal Weizman, Elizabeth Breiner, and Robert Trafford

FORENSIS

Forensis, the offshoot of the London agency founded in 2021, is a non-governmental, not-for-profit association based in Berlin. Drawing on techniques developed in an academic context, the team works for and in collaboration with individuals and communities affected by state and corporate violence to support their demands for justice, reparations, and accountability.

Project participants: Tobechukwu Onwukeme, Dimitra Andritsou, Phoebe Walton, Jasper Humpert, Miriam Rainer, and Veronika Nad

On February 24, 2022, Russia invaded Ukraine, following its attempts to seize the country since the annexation of the Crimean Peninsula in 2014. Mariupol, a city thirty-five miles from the eastern border, was besieged by Russian troops shortly after the invasion began. During the siege, the Donetsk Academic Regional Drama Theater in the center of Mariupol served as one of the largest civilian shelters in the city. On March 16, despite being clearly marked as a civilian shelter—the residents had drawn the Russian word ДЕТИ (CHILDREN) in two locations on the square outside the theater—the theater was destroyed by Russian forces, who allegedly hit it with two bombs.

The destruction and subsequent occupation of Mariupol by the Russian Armed Forces have fragmented its communities, leaving most survivors dispersed across different regions of Ukraine and other parts of Europe. This project investigates the bombing of the Mariupol Drama Theater as an emblem of Russia's many strategies of terror. The CST team aims to assemble the voices of members of the Mariupol Theater diaspora within a digital project of reconstruction. The detailed digital twin of the now-destroyed architecture is used as both a backdrop for situated testimonies and as a tool to locate visual material documenting the theater during the siege.

The CST team has collected and analyzed thousands of social media posts, photographs, and videos, in addition to recording over one hundred hours of interviews with witnesses of the air strike. With no access to the site and in light of the systematic destruction of both physical and digital evidence by the Russian military, these recollections constitute an essential historical document. The researchers identified sixty eyewitnesses of the events, twenty-seven of whom agreed to talk with them on record. Ten witnesses were invited to participate in further interview sessions using the "situated testimony"[1] technique developed by the CST's partnering organization, Forensic Architecture. This technique involves using 3D models of scenes and environments in which traumatic events occurred to aid in the process of interviewing and collecting testimony from

34   Case Study

Composite sketch and model of the theater, highlighting its various "zones" and how they were used by the self-organized inhabitants.

Video of the ruins of the Mariupol Theater being bulldozed behind scaffolding put up by Russian forces, overlaid on a 3D model.
Image source: Peter Andryushchenko, Telegram

CST's digital reconstruction of the theater enables precise geolocation of images and video stills sourced from residents of the theater within the model.

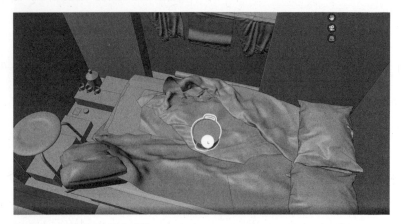

Witnesses worked with CST researchers to reconstruct intimate details of their living situations within the theater while they were residing there.

Scan the QR code for additional information and to watch full-length interviews with five witnesses.

witnesses. The collaborative reconstruction process allowed survivors to "walk through" the virtual space of the theater and model different aspects of the building as they remembered it. The resulting model documents both larger spatial reorganizations and smaller, individual interventions and objects.

The joint process facilitated recollection and helped the CST team fill in missing details in the digital model. As each witness recalled their part in this complex event, the model became an increasingly rich assemblage of collective and individual memory. The videos allow an understanding of how individual memories—some contradictory—result in a coherent image of the shared reality.

1   "Situated Testimony is a technique of interviewing developed by Forensic Architecture over the course of half a dozen projects, throughout our history. Situated testimony uses 3D models of the scenes and environments in which traumatic events occurred, to aid in the process of interviewing and gathering testimony from witnesses to those events. Memories of traumatic or violent episodes can often be elusive, or distorted, but we have found that the use of digital architectural models has a productive effect on a witness's recollection. Together with an architectural researcher, a witness is filmed reconstructing the scene of an event, exploring and accessing their memories of the episode in a controlled and secure manner." "Investigation Methodology: Situated Testimony," *Forensic Architecture,* https://forensic-architecture.org/methodology/situated-testimony

How Open Source Intelligence Improves Investigative Journalism

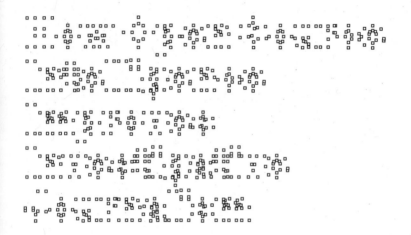

Lea Weinmann

LEA WEINMANN

Lea Weinmann has been an editor in the investigative team at the *Süddeutsche Zeitung* since 2022. She is responsible for online research and focuses on how open source intelligence (OSINT) can be used in journalism. She writes about war and crisis zones, cyber security, abuse of power, and MeToo cases. Before her traineeship at SZ, she studied cross-media editing in Stuttgart and worked as a freelance journalist, including for Südwestrundfunk, *Stuttgarter Zeitung,* and *Correctiv.* She has been awarded the Franco-German Journalism Prize and nominated for the German Reporter Award, among others. In 2024, she was voted one of the "Top 30 to 30" journalistic talents in Germany by *Medium Magazin.*

In April 2022, pictures of the corpses of Bucha circulated around the world. The dead lay in the middle of the street, some next to their bikes, some next to their shopping bags, some with their hands tied behind their backs. These images caused horror and disbelief about so much arbitrary violence, and ominous dread. The will to destroy must have raged in this suburb of Kyiv while the Russian troops had control of it.

On March 31, 2022, the Russians' control lagged. The soldiers retreated from Bucha. On the same day, pictures of the slain civilians surfaced on the internet. Many of the deceased had already died during the battles, for example in missile attacks. Others had been shot in the head or run over by tanks. About the same time the photos documenting these atrocities were taken, Russia's claim spread: the people in the street were not killed by Russian soldiers; they were placed there after the troops had moved out.

That, we now know, was a lie. It was part of a disinformation campaign in a war waged not only by tanks and missiles, but also with words, images, and emotions.

The task of journalists is to get as close to the truth as possible, amid all the chaos and outcry accompanying every war—as close as possible because nobody can be entirely objective at all times when viewing the world and reporting on it. Knowing this, and reflecting on it, is an essential part of our job. Nonetheless, it is our unconditional assignment to recognize disinformation and to call it by name.

In a world where information comes in thick and fast around the clock, and where it is hard for journalists to access war zones and crisis areas, this state of affairs is getting increasingly difficult: Who is lying? Who is telling the truth? What really happened? How do we figure it out, and as quickly as possible? Methods of open source intelligence (OSINT) have been helping journalism for some years, aiming to answer these exact questions—or at least get closer to an answer. The term OSINT is generally understood to cover all publicly accessible sources.

This includes pictures and videos on social media, databases, ships and aircraft carriers, public leaks, and internet archives—in short: everything legally obtainable on the internet.

In the case of the crimes of Bucha, satellite images that were published by *The New York Times* just a few days later revealed the lie put forth by the Ministry of Defence of the Russian Federation: they had been taken on different days in March 2022—all during a period when Russian troops were still in the area. At the exact spot where photographers would later find corpses in the street, little black dots were seen on the satellite images: dead bodies, at least eleven along Yablunska Street. They had to have been lying there since March 11.

The scene of Bucha is one of the main focuses of the investigation by the International Criminal Court because of the alleged war crimes in Ukraine since early 2022. Often investigators rely on pictures and videos nowadays; the war in Ukraine is considered to be one of the best documented in the world. This helps not only the justice system but also journalists.

OSINT methods are now also a part of the work at the German daily newspaper *Süddeutsche Zeitung,* especially in investigative research. There are numerous fields of application: satellite images, as well as pictures and videos from social media, help to document alleged war crimes but also aid in reporting on devastating events with great social or political implications. The media chronologically traced the storming of the US Capitol in January 2021 from various perspectives with the help of thousands of hours' worth of video material. The massacre at the Supernova Festival in Israel on October 7, 2023, is also documented in pictures and videos in all its brutality. Journalists use this visual material for extensive reconstruction—not to satisfy a lust for sensation, but so that nobody can reinterpret reality or turn a blind eye to what actually happened.

Look where others would apparently rather look away: we had one such case at the *Süddeutsche Zeitung* in the summer of 2022. At the end of June, several hundred migrants tried to overcome a border post with violence at the Spanish exclave Melilla in Africa. Melilla's border with Morocco is one of only two land borders between the European Union and Africa, and therefore also an EU external border. On that Friday morning, at least twenty-three people died at the border fence—under initially unresolved circumstances. Shortly thereafter, the German news agency dpa released a short report on the incident. It essentially stated that people had violently tried to enter the European Union, that Moroccan security forces had prevented them from doing so for the most part, and that some people had died. And Spain's Prime Minister Pedro Sánchez praised the "constructive cooperation" between Spanish and Morrocan border officials.

At the same time, more and more pictures and videos circulated on social media showing what had actually happened at the EU border that Friday morning. The recordings were brutal: irritant gas, people with sticks in hand, chaos, yelling. We saw and then also archived videos of bodies stacked on top of each other, of people suffocating on camera, and of police officers who beat people lying on the ground with batons. In the following days, our editorial staff tried to reconstruct what exactly had happened at the Melilla border. Why these people died—and what role the Morrocan border officials, so clearly praised by Sánchez, played in this.

After publishing our article, many questions remained unanswered, for instance exactly how many people had died, or why so many people were marching in the direction of the border at all. Nevertheless, our report delivered more information and enabled the public to conduct the political debates that ensued in a more informed way. All that was only possible with the help of the recordings from that day, which we verified and analyzed.

Verification means that we naturally refrained from using any untested pictures and videos for our report. We adhere to the same standards that ensure the quality of our reporting in general. In concrete terms, this means that we, for example, always geolocate pictures and videos, to find out precisely where they were taken. For this we use online map services, Street View data, and satellite images. It is also important to determine, as precisely as possible, when a recording was made. That is sometimes possible with metadata that is stored in a file. In other cases, we secure videos from other sources that show the same events from another perspective—in journalism, this procedure is called the two-source principle. And we of course have to rule out that a picture or video was manipulated. This is becoming increasingly difficult, but more on that later.

Reconstructions and research based on visual material are also referred to as "visual investigations." Especially *The New York Times* has shaped and driven this kind of research in recent years. Today, about twenty employees of the newspaper are active in the specially created Visual Investigations team. It was also *The New York Times* that tracked down the leaker of the Pentagon documents—using a tabletop. On a social media platform, they found a picture of the young man in military pants, and in the background a granite kitchen table was visible. The journalists already had clues based on other research that the man could be the leaker wanted by the FBI. The granite veins of the table in this photograph matched those of the leaked pictures, which gave the Visual Investigations team their final clue: shortly afterward, the research team rang Jack T.'s doorbell—a few hours before the FBI showed up as well.

Such spectacular research is sadly not a part of everyday journalism. Nevertheless, OSINT methods help, especially in investigative research, almost daily. Often in ways that are ultimately not even noticeable in the published report. In May 2024, for example, we reported on a video of the German island Sylt, which showed young people loudly blaring racist lines to the song "L'amours toujours" by Gigi D'Agostino and doing the Hitler salute in the background. The *SZ* was not the only organization reporting on this incident; the video went viral, and nearly all German media picked up on it. In our article, though, other attendees of the party had their say too. We found them on social media because they had released some videos of the Pentecost celebration on Sylt, furnished with placemarks or hashtags.

This is also OSINT: an opportunity to bring in another perspective, letting people speak who haven't been quoted everywhere already.

In other cases, online research helps us to verify information independently from sources. Even when a source confides in us, we still have to substantiate their claims to the best of our ability, before deciding to report on it. Recently, we conducted research about a UN soldier and had information indicating that he was to have been in an African country during a specific time frame. There was, however, no evidence to support this, no pictures, no documents. Then we found his public profile on a running app, which he had used to track all his jogging routes—including those in the African country, with the number of kilometers, duration, and exact date.

In my opinion, the best part about OSINT in investigative journalism is that you can make your research paths transparent. This is special because investigative journalists do not usually disclose how they obtained their information. For one, to protect their source—source protection is the highest commandment in our field of work. On the other hand, the content of the research—the poor state of affairs that we are denouncing—shouldn't take a back seat to the research itself. OSINT research is mostly based on public sources that can be named. Journalists often get accused of being controlled, operating in secret, following secret plans. To meet these conspiracy myths with more transparency in research is a chance that journalism should take full advantage of.

Of course, OSINT methods aren't a one-stop solution. A lot of research still runs into dead ends even when using all the OSINT tricks of the trade. Useful online tools sometimes lead in the wrong direction or suddenly don't work anymore. In addition, more—and deceptively real-looking—AI images and videos flood the web every day. How do we make sure that supposedly authentic images actually depict what they claim to show? That is a question that will occupy us more and more frequently and urgently in journalism. I myself have not found a satisfying answer yet. There is no "all-round tool" that can tell for sure if an image is real or artificially created, trustworthy or manipulated. So far, it is best to rely on your own wits and not on tools.

On the other hand, artificial intelligence can also improve OSINT research: various AI-supported online applications make it possible, for example, to geolocate an image much faster or even in a completely automated way. This saves time, which we can reinvest in research.

OSINT methods also have their limits. Journalists should never exclusively rely on tools and the internet. The best research on the web does not replace a personal conversation with a reliable source. However, OSINT research is not about replacing classic journalism at all. It can best be compared to a toolbox available to journalists: every tool stands for a research method. The opportunities of open source intelligence equate to an expansion of the toolbox. A few helpful tools have been added. All the same, journalists can and should not give up the hammer and chisel, that is, their telephone and notepad.

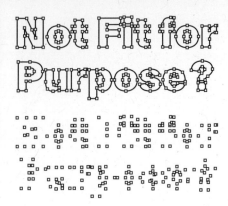

Climate Law, Science, Technology, and the People on the Frontlines

Anjli Parrin

ANJLI PARRIN

Anjli Parrin is a Kenyan human rights lawyer and assistant clinical professor of law at the University of Chicago Law School, where she directs the Global Human Rights Clinic. The Clinic works alongside partners and communities to advance justice and address the structural disparities that lead to human rights violations worldwide. Parrin conducts human rights fact-finding, investigations, research, and advocacy in the areas of armed conflict and international criminal law, colonialism and its impacts, climate justice, discrimination and inequality, and socio-economic rights. She is also an advisor to the UN Special Rapporteur on Extrajudicial, Summary, or Arbitrary Executions.

The tea farmers in Kenya, where I am from, for generations used to be able to accurately predict the start of the country's two annual rainy periods. Growing up, I would ask any of them, and they would look up and prophetically tell me, "in twelve days, it will start raining." They could also calculate the unpredictability of the rains; flooding and droughts have typically occurred along multiyear cycles.

Recently though, the rains haven't been quite the same. Droughts.[1] Then floods.[2] Followed by even more terrible flooding.[3] At unusual times of the year. Cold weather when it should be hot, and then sweltering heat waves the likes of which we couldn't have imagined. Which precipitates a huge influx of mosquitoes, driving me crazy at night when I try to sleep.[4] We have also had other changes related to those with whom we share our lands. Recently, we have had a beautiful red-winged Ross's turaco visit us at our home in Nairobi. → FIG. 1 And more and more monkeys. Timid ones, mischievous ones, families of monkeys with young babies. Incredible to look at, but I know that they are moving here because of changes in the climate and shifting patterns of biodiversity.

These are the small imprints of our burning planet.

It is a burning planet caused by what experts call the "triple planetary crisis"—of climate change, pollution, and biodiversity loss.[5]

Around the world, farmers, fisher persons, seafarers, medicine persons, and many others are observing similar changes to the waters and lands they depend upon. Fisher captains in Guam have told me that they have had to leave waters which they trawled for generations because the locations of the fish they catch have changed. Indigenous medicine persons can no longer find key plants they need for their practice that were once plentiful. Kayak tour guides in Alaska say that they can dramatically see the glaciers melting further and further each summer, collapsing into the heating ocean. → FIGS. 2 + 3

Figure 1.   Ross's turaco spotted in Nairobi.

Figure 2.   Alaska's glaciers are melting and collapsing into the heating ocean.

While we are all affected in small and large ways, the impacts of the triple planetary crisis are not felt equally. There are those on the frontlines—individuals living in small island nations, Indigenous groups, those in greater poverty, and those who have been historically (and still continue to be) systematically marginalized. So much so, that Tendayi Achiume, the former United Nations Special Rapporteur on contemporary forms of racism, racial discrimination, xenophobia, and related intolerance, has dubbed the climate crisis a "racial justice crisis," identifying what she calls "global 'sacrifice zones'—regions rendered dangerous and even uninhabitable due to environmental degradation."[6] Those who inhabit the "sacrifice zones" are residents of the world's small island nations, Indigenous groups, young people, and communities in the most vulnerable locations across the Global South. For these groups, discussions of climate change are quite literally existential.

The great irony is that these people who are at the frontier of the climate crisis are most frequently those who have contributed least to causing climate harm. Small island developing states contribute less than 1 percent of global greenhouse gas emissions.[7] In 2022, Kiribati—a small island nation in the Pacific—had thirty times less CO_2 emissions per capita than the United States, the country in which I now live.[8] Small island nations are drowning while rich states continue to pollute, largely unchecked.

LITIGATING THE CLIMATE CRISIS

Coalitions of young people around the world, led by those living at the frontier of the climate crisis, are pushing to ensure a livable present and future for all. Groups such as Pacific Island Students Fighting Climate Change (PISFCC), founded in 2019 by twenty-seven students from the University of the South Pacific, and the World's Youth for Climate Justice (WYCJ), a global coalition of young people, are documenting the harm caused by climate change, telling the stories of the impact on their homes, and advocating for urgent change and adaptation. Since 2019, PISFCC has been pushing to take the question of what is owed as a result of harm to the climate to the International Court of Justice (ICJ)—popularly known as the World's Court, which is charged with deciding matters between states. In March 2023, the students won the right to make their case.

The students teamed up with the Republic of Vanuatu, which brought together a coalition of 132 states to adopt a UN General Assembly resolution by consensus, asking the ICJ to rule on questions of climate change.[9] While the format of the case— an advisory opinion—is not binding on states, it nonetheless is extremely persuasive and frequently respected and followed. It often also indicates how future binding litigation relating to climate change is likely to proceed. The International Court of Justice has been tasked with answering three simple but key questions.[10]

First, what obligations do states have under international law to protect the climate for present and future generations? Second, what are consequences for states who cause harm to the climate with respect to other states, especially small island developing states, which are most vulnerable? Finally, what consequences should there be for states that cause harm to those peoples, both present and future generations, affected by the climate crisis? Essentially, these questions ask the court to tell us what countries must do to protect the climate, and what liabilities they will face if they cause harm. The questions also get at the inequality of who is most burdened, asking what small island developing states are specifically owed, as well as what countries owe individuals, now and in the future, who are harmed.

In recognition of the gravity of this case, in April 2024, the court announced that it had received ninety-one written submissions by its deadline, the highest number it has ever received for an advisory opinion.[11] States who have submitted now have the opportunity to comment once more in writing upon the submissions by others, with oral hearings likely taking place thereafter. A ruling will probably still take several months.

Figure 3. Rising sea level in Guam submerges low-lying areas, erodes beaches, and exacerbates coastal flooding from typhoons and tsunamis.

The ICJ advisory opinion is just one of a number of incredibly important advisory opinions which are deciding the trajectory of climate justice and liability for climate harm. In January 2023, Chile and Colombia brought a request to the Inter-American Court of Human Rights asking the court to clarify what the responsibilities of states within the inter-American system are to deal with climate emergencies.[12] In December 2022, a coalition of small island nations requested that the International Tribunal for the Law of the Sea (ITLOS) rule on the obligations of states to prevent, reduce, and control pollution of the marine environment caused by the effects of climate change.[13] Thus far, only the ITLOS has issued its ruling, finding in a landmark decision in May 2024 that states had duties to take specific, concrete steps to prevent harm to the marine environment, using the best available science.[14]

BETWEEN LAW, SCIENCE, AND PEOPLE

Activists and affected communities have tremendous hope that these advisory opinions will ensure some accountability for climate harm and lead to greater protection of the climate. And these efforts are incredibly vital, urgent, and necessary. However, on their own they are insufficient.

Over the coming years, lawyers will bicker in front of courts over science and causation, debating whether the latest devastating hurricane or extreme weather event can be attributed to climate change. Even though science has a consistent message, they will poke holes in the evidence. They will ask: When will the small islands whose people fought so hard to obtain answers before the World's Court, really sink? Is it really all that imminent? If all of these scientists cannot agree on what the *exact* effects of climate crisis will be and when they will occur, maybe it is not actually happening? How do we really know what is causing this all? And even if we know, can you really prove that my country or my company's emissions contributed to a wildfire thousands of miles away, or a house to be swept away by floods?

These are some of the inherent problems with law and science. Law is a backward-looking blunt instrument, premised on past harm. You steal my bicycle: I take you to court to recover its value. If you will steal my bicycle in the future, I cannot preemptively take you to court now. But what happens when the future harm is existential? What happens when our emissions and damage to the climate today mean that our future planet will be uninhabitable for most?

Our existing understandings of climate science, which often looks to disentangle past events and use this knowledge to predict the future, are also limiting, especially when applied in a courtroom. While science can help us to understand how multiple concepts like deforestation, pollution, loss of biodiversity, and global warming collectively will affect our future climate, it moves at a cautious pace, not necessarily tied to the urgency of the issues. Today, scientists are better able to understand the impact of anthropogenic changes to the Earth, but the knowledge systems are often still too general to be able to name the exact causes for specific climate events. Science works in probabilities, not absolutes. But courts want certainty; they want to be sure that harm has happened or will happen before punishing a specific person or entity and ordering that they provide reparative measures. So the challenge is how to reconcile all of the uncertainties that still remain in science with the certainty of someone who now has land that is no longer farmable or whose home was destroyed by extreme weather.

While these are real structural obstacles of law and science, they are the tools we have at our disposal to address climate justice. We need to show the court the voices, faces, and cultures and the forefront of the climate crisis, and what it means to live on the frontlines. We must also link contemporary climate injustice to the histories of violence and harm on their lands. The stories of the people who face the greatest harm—those losing their homes, lands, and livelihoods; entire countries facing imminent disappearance—turn climate litigation from abstract discussions of science, data, and state responsibility into real and human experiences which cannot be ignored.

The court also needs to hear about the ways in which communities are engaging in climate adaptation—methods relying upon ancestral knowledge of their lands and oceans to help preserve and protect them, alongside new technologies. This is critical in informing possible solutions, which the court will ultimately seek to provide to redress the harm.

One way to do this is to use visual investigations and documentary filmmaking as a storytelling tool to combine and distill narratives, data, science, and law. Visual investigations can help us to find complex scientific data about many of the indicators of climate change,[15] including rising sea levels, atmospheric CO_2, air and surface temperatures changes, ocean acidification, glaciers melting. This data can then be merged with the macro-level effects—such as flooding, extreme weather events, wildfires, changes in ocean environments, loss of arable land—and the micro-level impacts on specific individuals. Instead of thousands of pages of dry scientific reports, studies, and individual testimonies, we can see the harm directly and situate it within the respective historical context of colonialism, militarism, and extraction. This can be a tool not for providing answers, but for provoking discussion and debate.

Currently, at the Pinakothek der Moderne in Munich, SITU Research in Brooklyn, New York, and the Global Human Rights Clinic at the University of Chicago Law School, in partnership with the artist Suneil Sanzgiri, the students at the PISFCC and the WYCJ are aiming to do just this. We have developed a film drawing on the visual investigations methodology to showcase what is at stake in the ICJ advisory opinion, and the particular impact that frontline communities in small island nations in the Pacific are facing. By using art to merge scientific data, law, and the stories of lived experiences, we can help make these cases more accessible and easier to understand. → FIGS. 4 + 5

We know that, ultimately, the conversation cannot simply end in the courts. We all need to participate, to critically examine how the processes work and who is impacted most. We need to dissect and analyze the judgments. We should discuss them in

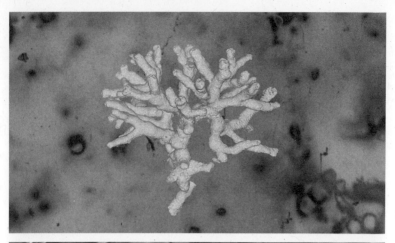

Figures 4 and 5.   Suneil Sanzgiri's film merges scientific data, law, and stories of lived experience.

classrooms, and even in museums. We can start conversations about what is already happening, and what more is needed.

With climate justice, everything at stake is existential. This is already the hard reality of the people on the frontlines of climate change, and will become everyone else's reality in the near future. We owe it to them today, and to all of us tomorrow, to rise to the challenge.

Author's Note

I am incredibly grateful to Ryan Manzuk, Candice Strongwater, and Priyanka Motaparthy for their comments on this essay, and to Brad Samuels and the entire SITU Research team for their vision, innovations, and contributions to advancing climate justice through visual investigations.

1. UN Office for the Coordination of Humanitarian Affairs, "Kenya Drought Response Dashboard (May 2022)," https://www.unocha.org/publications/report/kenya/kenya-drought-response-dashboard-may-2022.

2. UN Office for the Coordination of Humanitarian Affairs, "Kenya: Heavy Rains and Floods Impact and Response (as of 20 December 2023)," https://www.unocha.org/publications/report/kenya/kenya-heavy-rains-and-floods-impact-and-response-20-december-2023.

3. Agence France-Presse, "Kenya Floods Death Toll at 228 as Crisis Persists," *Voice of America (VOA)*, May 5, 2024, https://www.voanews.com/a/kenya-floods-death-toll-at-228-as-crisis-persists/7598540.html.

4. Bethlehem Feleke and Larry Madowo, "Kenya's Hard Won Gains against Malaria Threatened by Surging Temperatures," CNN, September 7, 2023, https://www.cnn.com/2023/09/07/africa/malaria-mosquitoes-kenya-climate-change-intl/index.html.

5. United Nations Climate Change, "What Is the Triple Planetary Crisis?," April 13, 2022, https://unfccc.int/news/what-is-the-triple-planetary-crisis.

6. UN Office of the High Commissioner for Human Rights, "The Global Climate Crisis Is a Racial Justice Crisis: UN Expert," October 31, 2022, https://www.ohchr.org/en/press-releases/2022/11/global-climate-crisis-racial-justice-crisis-un-expert. The Special Rapporteur released a report on ecological crisis, climate justice, and racial justice. See UN General Assembly, A/77/549, October 25, 2022.

7. United Nations Department of Economic and Social Affairs, "Small Islands Prepare for Their Big Moment in 2024," January 19, 2024, https://www.un.org/en/desa/small-islands-prepare-their-big-moment-2024.

8. Our World in Data, "Per Capita CO2 Emissions," https://ourworldindata.org/grapher/co-emissions-per-capita?tab=table.

9. Vanuatu ICJ Initiative, https://www.vanuatuicj.com.

10. UN General Assembly, A/RES/77/276, April 4, 2023.

11. International Court of Justice, "Obligations of States in Respect of Climate Change (Request for Advisory Opinion), Filing of Written Statements," press release, April 12, 2024, https://www.icj-cij.org/sites/default/files/case-related/187/187-20240412-pre-01-00-en.pdf.

12. International Tribunal for the Law of the Sea, "Request for an Advisory Opinion submitted by the Commission of Small Island States on Climate Change and International Law (Request for Advisory Opinion submitted to the Tribunal)," advisory opinion, May 21, 2024.

13. "Request for an advisory opinion on climate emergency and human rights to the Inter-American Court of Human Rights from the Republic of Colombia and the Republic of Chile," January 9, 2023.

14. Catherine Amirfar and Duncan Pickard, "Q&A: 'The Oceans Court' Issues Landmark Advisory Opinion on Climate Change," *Just Security,* May 21, 2024, https://www.justsecurity.org/95874/itlos-advisory-opinion-climate-change/.

15. The Global Climate Observing System (GCOS) has identified key indicators to understand climate-related changes to the atmosphere, land, and ocean, which go beyond simply rising temperatures. For its regular reports and analysis, see GCOS, "Global Climate Indicators," https://gcos.wmo.int/en/global-climate-indicators.

What Is Owed?

Taking the Climate Crisis to the World Court

SITU Research, New York City, in collaboration with the University of Chicago's Global Human Rights Clinic, Pacific Island Students Fighting Climate Change, World's Youth for Climate Justice, and Suneil Sanzgiri

2023–ongoing

SITU RESEARCH, SEE PAGE 27

Project participants: Brad Samuels, Candice Strongwater, and Ryan Manzuk, PhD Candidate at the Department of Geoscience, Princeton University

THE UNIVERSITY OF CHICAGO LAW SCHOOL'S GLOBAL HUMAN RIGHTS CLINIC

The University of Chicago Law School's Global Human Rights Clinic (GHRC) works alongside partners and communities to advance justice and address the inequalities and structural disparities that lead to human rights violations worldwide. The GHRC uses diverse tactics and interdisciplinary methods to tackle pressing and under-addressed human rights issues and to train the next generation of effective, ethical, and creative lawyers. The work of the clinic includes investigating mass atrocities, pushing for climate justice, addressing the impacts of colonialism, advocating for equality and non-discrimination, and advancing socioeconomic rights.

Project participants: Anjli Parrin, Michelle Esposito, and Sarah Ginsburg

PACIFIC ISLAND STUDENTS FIGHTING CLIMATE CHANGE

Pacific Island Students Fighting Climate Change (PISFCC) are a coalition of lawyers, activists, and students from the Pacific Islands who are seeking climate justice at the International Court of Justice (ICJ). They are demanding that the court respond to a legal question to develop international law, integrate legal obligations around environmental treaties and basic human rights and clarify state responsibility for climate harm.

Project participants: Vishal Prasad, Siosiua Veikune, and Sonia Jitt

WORLD'S YOUTH FOR CLIMATE JUSTICE

World's Youth for Climate Justice (WYCJ) is a global youth-led campaign to take climate change and human rights to the ICJ to seek an advisory opinion. In 2020, standing in solidarity with the PISFCC and recognizing that global support was needed to obtain an advisory opinion on climate change from the ICJ, youth from Asia, Africa, the Caribbean, Latin America, and Europe organized as WYCJ. On March 29, 2023, the United Nations General Assembly (UNGA) responded to the call of the young people and the leadership of Vanuatu by adopting, by consensus, a resolution requesting the advisory opinion from the ICJ. This overwhelming support shows the significance of youth-led climate justice initiatives and its impact across the globe. WYCJ seeks to convince states from within and beyond respective national boundaries to protect the rights of present and future generations from the adverse effects of climate change.

Project participants: Samira Ben Ali, Yasmin Bijvank, and Jule Schnakenberg

SUNEIL SANZGIRI

Suneil Sanzgiri is an artist, researcher, and filmmaker, born in Dallas, Texas, in 1989 and currently living in Brooklyn, New York. His work spans experimental video and film, animations, essays, and installations and contends with questions of identity, heritage, culture, and diaspora in relation to structural violence.

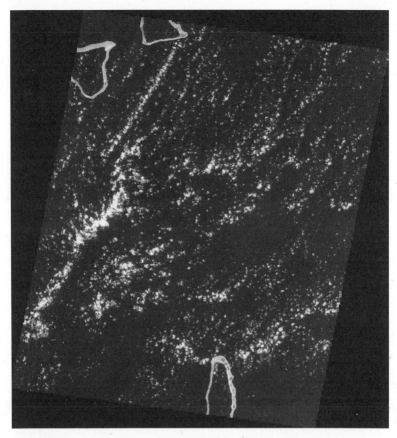

The Marshall Islands are just one of the many atolls in the South Pacific that are highly vulnerable to the rise in sea level and other impacts of climate change. As seen from a RapidEye satellite image © 2016, Planet Labs PBC.

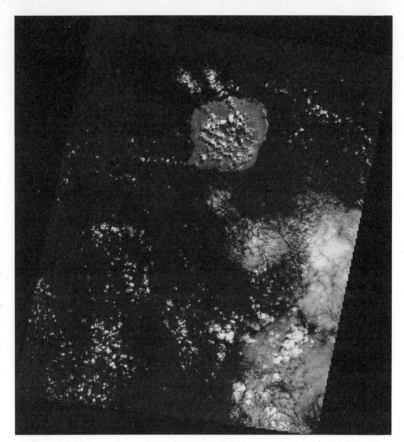

Vanuatu is one of the countries most at risk from climate-related natural disasters. As seen from a RapidEye satellite image © 2016, Planet Labs PBC.

People on the frontlines of the climate crisis are frequently those who have contributed least to climate harms—including Indigenous groups, individuals living in small island nations, and communities across the Global South. In many spaces, the corrosive transnational forces of the climate crisis are exacerbated by unfettered fossil fuel emissions, military buildup, and the legacies and ongoing impacts of colonial expansion.

While climate scientists, legal scholars, and world leaders debate the extent of the climate crisis and how to mitigate it, coalitions of young people have been working together to take action on their own, refusing to let their homes disappear. In particular, the Pacific Island Students Fighting Climate Change and World's Youth for Climate Justice are making the argument that the right to a livable present and future is not only at stake, but should be protected under international law.

For these students, who are already experiencing the acute effects of climate change, the time to act is now. In March 2023, working with the government of Vanuatu, they succeeded in getting a historic resolution adopted, asking the International Court of Justice (ICJ)—the "World's Court"—to rule on the obligations owed by top violators due to climate inaction. Catalyzed by this youth movement, initial submissions have been sent to the Court, and hearings will presumably take place in December 2024.[1] While the case is ongoing in the ICJ courtroom, these youth activists are continuing to document the harms, speak out, protest, research climate adaptation plans, and litigate around the world.

Over the past decade, efforts to redress climate harms have more often than not been paralyzed in an impasse between the logic of science and the logic of law. How do we measure harm to future generations? What constitutes a consensus within the scientific community with regard to imminence? Where do we draw the lines between weather and climate? How can we provide legal compensation today for tomorrow's harms? And how do we decide who caused climate harm that is often felt thousands of miles away? With few legal precedents and structural limitations within legal systems, those most directly impacted wait—while their homes disappear—for the law and science to catch up with their lived reality.

As part of these activist-led efforts, a film installation will debut in autumn 2024 at the Architecture Museum of the TUM, showing the lived experiences of communities on the frontlines of the climate crisis in the context of island nations in the South Pacific. Developed in close collaboration with artist and experimental filmmaker Suneil Sanzgiri, the short film weaves together a wide range of visual evidence, from archival footage in the Pacific Islands to 3D renderings, remote sensing, testimonies from activists, and more. The film works to expose the inherent colonial conditions of the ICJ—past and present—and the struggle for survival of Indigenous peoples across the Pacific Islands.

As renowned writer Epeli Hau'ofa states: "There is a world of difference between viewing the Pacific as 'islands in a far sea' and as 'a sea of islands.' The first emphasizes dry surfaces in a vast ocean far from the centers of power. Focusing in this way stresses the smallness and remoteness of the islands. The second is a more holistic perspective in which things are seen in the totality of their relationships."[2]

The film brings you into that sea of islands and shows you the ocean peoples for whom it is home and who are fighting for its survival. Scan the QR code on page 67 to watch the full-length film.

---

1   Note from the editors: This is the current state of knowledge at the time of writing (August 2024). Via the QR code, you will be able to access up-to-date information on the outcome of the hearings at a later date. At this stage, we do not yet know when this will be, so please scan the code from time to time for updates.

2   Epeli Hau'ofa, "Our Sea of Islands," *The Contemporary Pacific* 6, no. 1 (Spring 1994): 148–61, https://www.jstor.org/stable/23701593.

   Epeli Hau'ofa (1939–2009) was born in Papua New Guinea and educated in Papua New Guinea, Tonga, Fiji, Australia, and Canada. He worked at the University of the South Pacific's main campus in Suva, Fiji, where he was the founder and director of the Oceania Centre for Arts and Culture, established in 1997.

Suneil Sanzgiri's short film merges different kinds of visual evidence such as archival video footage, satellite imagery, and activists' testimony to create a compelling picture of the lived experience of communities in the South Pacific.

Scan the QR code for additional information and to watch the full-length film.

Taking the Climate Crisis to the World Court 67

Empowering Critical Literacy

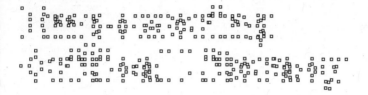

Laura Kurgan [LK] in Conversation with
Andres Lepik [AL]

LAURA KURGAN

Laura Kurgan teaches spatial information design, data visualization, and critical cartography at Columbia University's Graduate School of Architecture, Planning and Preservation (GSAPP), where she is a professor of architecture and directs the program M.S. Computational Design Practices. She founded the Spatial Information Design Lab at GSAPP in 2004, which was succeeded by the Center for Spatial Research in 2015. Her research and creative work emphasize hands-on critical engagement with spatial technologies in the areas of conflict and injustice. She has written *Close Up at a Distance: Mapping, Technology, and Politics* (2013) and coedited *Ways of Knowing Cities* (2019).

ANDRES LEPIK, SEE PAGE 15

ANDRES LEPIK   Satellites have been documenting changes on Earth for over half a century and the amount of data being processed on the ground is constantly growing. The ability to view transformation remotely is an achievement—yet it should not be celebrated as a savior without some reservations. What opportunities does remote sensing technology bring to the field of visual investigations, and what limitations do we need to be aware of?

LAURA KURGAN   I would like to start answering this question by defining my understanding of the term "visual investigation." For me, it refers a relatively recent turn in journalism toward investigative storytelling and research through visual communication with data. But on a larger scale, it also describes the development of a field that has become more and more important over the last fifteen years and has been (and continues to be) guided by practices such as Forensic Architecture, as well as the artists in your show. *The New York Times,* for example, has only had its Visual Investigations department since 2017, but as early as 1999 it published high-resolution before-and-after satellite images of Grozny, Chechnya, as evidence that a huge part of the city had been destroyed in a series of Russian attacks.

Satellite imagery and technology have had two main reasons for coming into being: the low-resolution satellites, for example the Landsat missions launched by the United States from 1972 onward, were about environmental monitoring. Crewed space missions also generated a lot of images. In my 2013 book *Close Up at a Distance,* I discuss the first views of the Earth from the moon and what it meant to look at the Earth from space. These images were enormously important not simply for research but for generating a popular consciousness about "Spaceship Earth." The impression left by that view of Earth was utopian. It was the image of a world beyond politics, beyond borders—Earth as an unlimited globe that holds all people together in a sort of beautiful unity. Now, Landsat imagery is freely downloadable by anyone in the world. That's one aspect.

On the other hand, and at the same time, there were satellites with high-resolution image capabilities, which were classified secrets and were used for military and intelligence surveillance operations. These were about looking at the Earth from space in order to see what other governments were doing, and then using this information for military, economic, and political purposes.

In my work, too, I've followed the uses of both high- and low-resolution imagery. Where military intelligence images are concerned, I focused on its inadvertent uses— if you will, a flip side—of surveillance: memory. Satellite imagery are snapshots in space and time. Today, satellite imagery is used for many purposes, by civilians, corporations, and governments, but there are limitations based on the ownership of the technology. Whoever owns the technology is often the one who controls the technology. For example, even though private companies own high-resolution commercial satellites right now, the US military has the potential to invoke what they call "shutter control." They had the power to temporarily ban purchases of high-resolution satellite images of Iraq in 2002, for example, claiming at the time that it was protecting a view of US military operations. This happened to me when I was trying to purchase satellite imagery in the mid-2000s. And then, of course, there are technological thresholds and limits, like the pixel resolution, which is something I followed in my early work as higher and higher resolution imagery became available.

AL   The technologies that research teams work with when using visual investigation are subject to constant improvement. You have been leading the Center for Spatial Research at Columbia University's Graduate School for Architecture, Planning and Preservation since 2015, and you have been working on the contextualization of geo-related data for over thirty years. How does today's work with remotely generated data differ from back then?

LK   When I started my research, I first got to work with the Global Positioning System (GPS).[1] The accuracy of the signal in those days was still rather fuzzy for civilians, and it took some clever hacking to overcome the scrambling. GPS nerds would build local "base stations" at known locations, which made it possible to correct the drifting readings that the GPS receiver—which back then was the size of a suitcase—would produce. When I did the 1995 show *You Are Here* at MACBA,[2] for example, there was already a base station installed in Barcelona, so I could take advantage of it to get more accurate information from my GPS receiver by measuring and correcting the errors in its readings.

In terms of satellite imagery, back when I started doing my work, a lot of the pictures were still classified—especially all one-meter-resolution and under-resolution images. A big part of my first book dealt with the questions of how and when this data became accessible. In 1999, when images of sites of war crimes committed in Kosovo were released to a global public, they were just pictures, not data. The handout photos were illustrative, images of mass graves stripped of longitude, latitude, and timestamps. → FIG.1 I went through all kinds of measures trying to restore the data to the public images, first by cross-referencing satellite images with other publicly released images (particularly from drones), corroborating features in the images with those found on maps, and finally by purchasing my own satellite images of the area at much lower resolutions than those the US military had released. → FIG.2 Based on what I found, I added thousands of small pixels (thanks to Photoshop) to the highest-resolution image I could obtain and was able to determine, by overlaying my shape onto the NATO imagery's shape, that they were in fact the same, and with that, I could precisely geo-locate the grave. → FIGS. 3–6 Twenty years later, I went

Figure 1. "Assessment photograph of grave tampering near Izbica, Kosovo, used by Assistant Secretary of Defense for Public Affairs Ken Bacon during a press briefing on NATO Operation Allied Force in the Pentagon on June 9, 1999." Caption and photo: US Department of Defense.

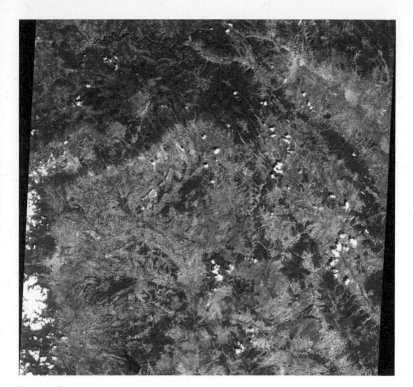

Figure 2.
kosovo: sat·k-j id·date·time·camera·sensor
SPOT Scene: 4·082-264·99/06/06/·09:32:30·1·m
Cloud cover: 0-10%
Extents: 38,834,152 pixels
Top left: 43°01'13" n, 20°21'17" e
Bottom right: 42°23'34" n, 20°55'22" e
Coverage: 64.81 × 59.92 kilometers
Resolution: 1 pixel = 10 meters
Includes material © 1999 spot image, all rights reserved

there, to visit the memorial site and read the names of the people who were buried there—it was a very sobering moment.

Today, investigators do not need to go through such a process, because you can access imagery of half-a-meter resolution, or even less, 42 centimeters per pixel. Over the course of thirty years, satellite imagery and all kinds of other satellite technologies have become declassified and are available to civilians. This shift enables citizens to check in on their governments and vice versa—if you have the money to purchase the imagery, since that is no small cost, and the basic skills to work with it.

AL So access to satellite images means buying them?

LK In most cases, yes! It still amazes me that more than ten years after my book was written, and after all the work that has been done on the topic by others, people still don't understand that Google Earth is not the actual provider of satellite imagery. Google purchases satellite imagery from private companies. If you open *The Washington Post* or any other newspaper in the United States and see a high-resolution satellite image, it most likely comes from Maxar. Maxar is a US-based company that owns nearly all the rights to satellite imagery these days. You can use Google Earth to figure out what you want to look at, but if you actually want to work with the data, you need to buy it. You go to the Maxar website and type in the longitude and latitude of the location you want to study. In doing that, you are "tasking" the satellite, literally. You will most likely specify that you would like a 100 percent cloudless image—and then you will wait. The satellite goes around and around, capturing your image on each revolution, and when the image is finally cloudless, then you purchase it and are able to download it. And when you do that, it gets stored in an archive and anyone else can buy the image that you have specifically tasked. They keep the tasker's identity private, though, so you never know who started looking in the first place: Laura Kurgan, the US government, the Federal Security Service of the Russian Federation (FSB), or anyone else.

AL In your 2013 publication *Close Up at a Distance,* the book you mentioned earlier, you state that "maps are never neutral," as they are always developed with an intention, or at least from a certain perspective. What role does architecture play in the contextualization of geo-related data?

LK That is a tricky question. I might have to push back on the question a little bit because I think geo-related data already includes architecture. You are defining architecture as only buildings, right? But as we can probably agree on (both in teaching and curating): today architecture is defined a lot more broadly, whether it's because we are questioning the Anthropocene, or not so sure about the line between digital and physical space, or for many other reasons. So many other things define the environments that make architecture possible, like infrastructure or soil or microbes or animals or anything that can be sensed by a satellite, or any other sensor for that matter. They form other kinds of intelligence. I don't know if architecture or buildings really play a role in the contextualization of geo-related data. I would argue for the other way around: geo-related data puts various forms of architecture in relation to one another. The physical and the virtual are so intertwined and mixed up nowadays. I'm not sure how anybody makes a distinction.

AL We definitely agree on a very broad definition of the term architecture! But let me rephrase the question: What role do architects play when they are no longer just viewed as planners of buildings, but as spatial researchers?

LK Architects are specialists of the built environment. And that is why what we learn in architecture school is very useful in visual investigations. My students are hired by visual investigations teams because they have the ability

76   Laura Kurgan in Conversation with Andres Lepik

Figure 3.
German cl 289 drone imagery of probable graves at Izbica, Kosovo, May 1999. Originally published on a Bundeswehr web page of "Drohnen-Bilder," reproduced at John Pike's Federation of American Scientists archive, "Kosovo Operation Allied Force Imagery," now at GlobalSecurity.org

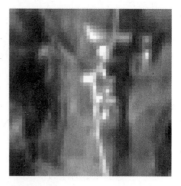

Figure 4.
kosovo: sat·k-j id·date·time·camera·sensor
SPOT Scene: 4·082-264·99/06/06/·09:32:30·1·m
Extents: 2,500 pixels
Top left: 42°43'47.81" n, 20°38'11.62" e
Bottom right: 42°42'9.47" n, 20°41'7.87" e
Coverage: 500 × 500 meters
Resolution: 1 pixel = 10 meters
Izbica, Kosovo, June 6, 1999

Figure 5.
kosovo: sat·k-j id·date·time·camera·sensor
SPOT Scene: 4·082-264·99/06/06/·09:32:30·1·m
Extents: 100 pixels
Top left: 42°43'45.76" n, 20°39'37.96" e
Bottom right: 42°43'41.98" n, 20°39'41.48" e
Coverage: 100 × 100 meters
Resolution: 1 pixel = 10 meters
Grave site, Izbica, Kosovo, June 6, 1999

Figure 6.
kosovo: sat·k-j id·date·time·camera·sensor
SPOT Scene: 4·082-264·99/06/06/·09:32:30·1·m
Extents: 10,562,500 pixels, enhanced from 100 pixels
Top left: 42°43'45.76" n, 20°39'37.96" e
Bottom right: 42°43'41.98"n, 20°39'41.48" e
Coverage: 100 × 100 meters
Resolution: enhanced to 1 pixel = 3 centimeters
Grave site, Izbica, Kosovo, June 6, 1999

to think about and visualize spaces of all sorts in a myriad of forms and formats. If you consider the education process of journalists, they are taught various things. They are taught to have a beat, a specific field of expertise (environment, criminal justice, etc.), and with that they are taught how to look at a local condition. Architects are taught those kinds of things as well, but they are presented with a set of very specific visual and analytic tools and habits of mind—apart from being a human and therefore having a visual sensibility and being able to communicate by asking questions. They are, for example, able to model the built environment and then interpret particular events, of whatever duration, through that model. That is why maps are not neutral. Drawings aren't neutral either. All of these things come with an investigative perspective.

AL   Today, satellite images are often shown in media coverage of current conflicts in order to visualize human rights violations. Many news channels use satellite data to verify and classify video and image material circulating on social media. How do you perceive this "trend"?

LK   Human Rights Watch, Amnesty International, and various UN agencies were among the first organizations to use satellite imagery in their investigations, especially in their work on war crimes starting in the early 2000s. This is why a lot of people associate working with satellite and open source material with human rights, but there are many other types of investigations making use of those technologies. The work of Forensic Architecture and the artists contributing to your exhibition shows that it can be very successful. No upstanding major media organization is without its own—or at least access to—a visual investigation team these days. Groups like Bellingcat have demonstrated that investigations do not have to be done only by professionals, thanks to the wide availability of social media imagery and the power that citizen investigators have to develop tools and skills and to teach them quickly to others. But that "democratization" does come with risks—governments can do it, too, as can human rights violators themselves, along with those who just want to introduce noise and confusion and endless skepticism into the political ecosystem.

AL Where do you see the greatest impact of your research to date?

LK I always have such a hard time with that kind of question. Perhaps the strongest impact that I've had is following these technologies for such a long period of time, while always looking for their potential limits as well as their uses. I try to follow trends and look for the dangers and the potentials in technology. I'm not someone who would say, "AI is evil—you should not use it at all." You have to figure out how to take technology back from the corporations who are trying to push it in one direction and push it in another. In my work, I am always finding inadvertent uses for technology and a form of critique without shying away from something. Working at a university, having my own labs and centers, gives me the freedom to choose my own research, because I am an academic. In this context I can direct topics that I think are important in terms of spatial technologies. And in my role as a teacher as well as in my work, I have taught this critical vision of technology. I think of what I am teaching not only as "counter cartography" or "critical cartography," but as a kind of visual and data literacy. Does that answer the question?

AL It does, and it's a great answer. I have the feeling that you are reaching and influencing the next generation through this type of educational work. Where do you see the discipline now and where do you think it is going?

LK There is no inside and outside of technology anymore. When I started working thirty years ago, the World Wide Web was launched. There was cyberspace which you could enter, and you could "escape." The promise was that one could free oneself from the constraints of the world—although that was never entirely true. Now there is no more inside and outside. You are directed everywhere by your cell phone and Google Maps and all the things that have become utilities of everyday life.

AL This leads me to a last question. In the future, who do you think will have control over all of this information? We see a lot of censorship happening all over the world. The utopia of "free Wi-Fi" or "free access" to all information never came true. And we can see a lot of countries regulating and limiting access. Where do you think this is going? And who is going to have control over this technology in the future?

LK You are asking two different questions. I'll start with who has control: the governments and corporations that are able to switch on and off the internet. That—for me—is about democracy. We have to fight for control. We have to fight for the internet as a global public utility. One of the reasons we got to the point where democracy is under threat to the extent it is today is because of the way that the infrastructure of the internet has been designed. Multibillion dollar companies, which provide access to the internet for free, allow anyone willing to pay to track so many things about you so they can know and predict most of your behavior, economic or political or social.

We need to campaign to take back the internet as a public infrastructure and as a public good. I would never equate it to oxygen, as some people do, or oil, which is the flip side of it in the capitalist world. But I think as a means of communication, like electricity and telephones, it is something we really have to fight to redesign in a different way. There are many places in the world where people are trying to remake and rethink things like Twitter and Facebook, major communication platforms. That would go a long way toward improving many more things!

1   GPS is US-owned utility based on twenty-four satellites and four ground stations that transmit highly accurate location data, which can be accessed by any portable receiver.

2   The installation *You Are Here* by Laura Kurgan was on display at the Museu d'Art Contemporani de Barcelona (MACBA) from November 30, 1995, to February 25, 1996. It was based on research about the presence of contemporary location and positioning information technologies as applied to architecture. Laura Kurgan produced graphics and drawings that were specific to the MACBA building and at the same time encouraged reflection on the fundamental activities of architecture: drawing, representing, and interpreting a place.

Investigating Xinjiang's Network of Detention Camps

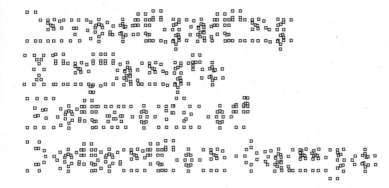

Alison Killing, Megha Rajagopalan, and Christo Buschek for BuzzFeed News

2018–20

ALISON KILLING

Alison Killing is an architect and investigative journalist who uses her architectural and urban planning expertise to address pressing human rights and social justice issues. In 2010, she established Killing Architects, a studio that focuses on both design and research in architecture. Killing employs innovative design strategies to effectively communicate the narratives uncovered in her investigations. In 2023, she joined the visual investigations team of the *Financial Times* as a senior reporter.

MEGHA RAJAGOPALAN

Megha Rajagopalan is an investigative reporter at *The New York Times,* operating out of London. Her journalistic focus is on issues related to human rights, labor, and conflicts. Before joining *The New York Times,* Rajagopalan was a key figure at BuzzFeed News, where she served as the China bureau chief and covered various regions in Asia. Additionally, she has extensive experience as a political correspondent for Reuters in Beijing, where she reported on diplomatic and security matters.

CHRISTO BUSCHEK

Christo Buschek is a programmer and digital security specialist dedicated to supporting investigative journalism and human rights advocacy. He focuses on creating custom tools that enhance the capabilities of data journalists and human rights defenders, enabling them to carry out secure and effective investigations.

Since late 2016, it is estimated that over one million Muslims have been imprisoned in a secretive network of detention camps and prisons in Xinjiang, China. This campaign of state surveillance, abuse, imprisonment, and religious suppression has been described as a genocide by governments such as those of the Netherlands and the UK and by experts and human rights groups.

The Uyghurs are the largest people group affected, but the crackdown also targets Kazakhs, Uzbeks, Kyrgyz, Hui, Mongols, Xibe, and other Indigenous people in the region. The Chinese government has claimed that the camps were part of a benign educational program designed to combat "extremism." In reality, however, people have been detained, sometimes for years, for religious expression or any behavior perceived to be disloyal, such as downloading WhatsApp, growing a beard, or studying abroad. Many people describe being taken away in the middle of the night, hooded and in chains, to terrifying prisons in unfamiliar locations.

At the start of this investigation in 2018, it was believed that there were 1,200 camps in existence, though only a few dozen had been discovered. Little was known about the network of camps or the locations to which the missing people had been taken. The findings of the investigative team, consisting of an architect, a journalist, and a software developer, significantly contributed to the understanding of this issue. These findings were published by BuzzFeed News and presented as a film installation at the Architecture Biennale in Venice in 2023.

The film is composed of eight chapters, in which Alison Killing, Megha Rajagopalan, and Christo Buschek present their research project "Built to Last." They describe their methodology and conclusions to create a foundation on which others can build, as is common in the field of open source intelligence (OSINT).

In order to find the camps, they mapped a series of masking tiles on Baidu's mapping platform (the Chinese equivalent of Google Maps) and then they looked at these same locations on

84   Case Study

Masked tile on Baidu Maps

Investigating Xinjiang's Network of Detention Camps

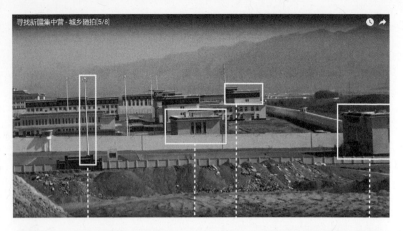

The team was able to cross-check distinctive features of architecture found on satellite imagery with amateur video footage of one of the camps.

86   Case Study

Google Earth, where the imagery was clearly available, to see what existed in that location. In this way the team was able to find 348 compounds in Xinjiang bearing the characteristics of prisons and internment camps and identify what researchers believe is close to the complete network of camps in the region.

The interface built by the team to analyze the resulting database enabled them to work through the mask tile locations systematically and create an annotated dataset of suspected camp locations. To verify these findings, the team spoke to former detainees who had managed to escape the region. In the interviews, they relate their memories of the camps, map them out, and even localize them geographically. Further corroboration of camp locations came from government documents and media reports.

In 2020, the team published their findings, including a map of all the camps, categorized by the degree of certainty as to their identity (e.g., "locations identified or corroborated by other sources, satellite images show perimeter walls and guard towers, likely used for detention in the past but now closed or reduced security"). In this regard, verification through witness statements and the unambiguousness of architectural elements played a particularly important role. To better understand the detention network and life inside the camps, the team created a detailed, digital 3D model of the detention complex in Mongolkure. They also obtained copies of the Chinese prison building regulations.

Based on this analysis, the team was able to conclude that the network of detention camps in Xinjiang has the capacity to hold over one million people—enough to imprison one in twenty-five of Xinjiang's population.

In 2021, the investigation team was awarded the Pulitzer Prize for International Reporting.

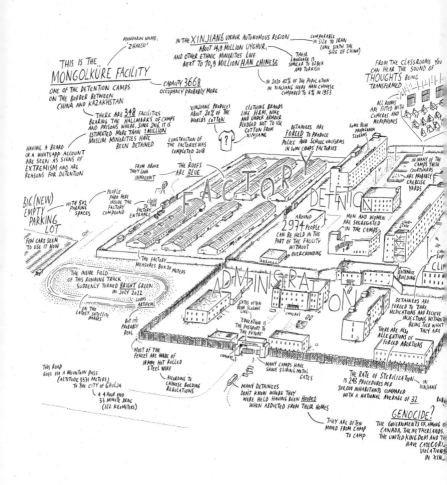

Camp on the road to Ghulja, Mongolkure
The information about this camp came from interviews with three former detainees held there, satellite imagery, the Chinese prison building regulations, reports by the UN and Amnesty International, and leaked documents reported on by the International Committee for Investigative Journalists and Adrian Zenz.

Case Study

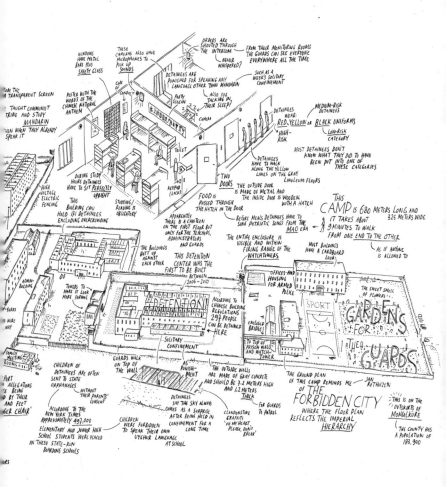

Scan the QR code on page 90 to zoom in on the drawing by Jan Rothuizen.

Investigating Xinjiang's Network of Detention Camps

In 2023, the research published on BuzzFeed News was exhibited as a film installation at the 18th International Architecture Exhibition of the Venice Biennale, *The Laboratory of the Future*, alongside a mural by Jan Rothuizen and a photographic series by Ekaterina Anchevskaja.

Project participants: Alison Killing, Megha Rajagopalan, Christo Buschek, Shumi Bose, Jan Rothuizen, Ekaterina Anchevskaya, Tanja Busking, and Anna Moreno

Scan the QR code for additional information, such as the drawing by Jan Rothuizen and the photographic series by Ekaterina Anchevskaya.

The pictures of Baqytali Nur and Nurlan Kokteubai are part of a series of photographs by Ekaterina Anchevskaya of former detainees of the camps in Xinjiang, China, and were taken in Almaty, Kazakhstan, in January 2020.

The Violent Image, Tunnel Vision, and Blind Faith

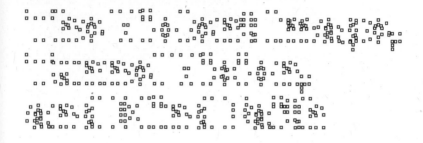

Reflections on the Argumentative Potency
of Visual Investigations

Bora Erden

BORA ERDEN

Bora Erden is a spatial researcher based in Turtle Island, known today as the United States of America. At *The New York Times,* he applies geospatial, computational, and investigative techniques on the Graphics desk. Previously at SITU Research, he provided forensic evidence to national and international judicial, advocacy, journalistic, and activist organizations. His work has been commissioned by Amnesty International, Human Rights Watch, the International Criminal Court, United Nations mechanisms, the Associated Press, and the Equipo Argentino de Antropología Forense, among others.

INTRODUCTION

My current occupation requires me, among other tasks, to write alt text for photographs, videos, diagrams, and maps included in articles. My job is to write a description of the media's contents, the obvious visual features that draw the eye, and the main information that is conveyed visually, so that people with vision impairments can have the description read to them through a screen reader. However, I have been told that my alt text is often too wordy, that it goes into secondary details that are not obvious to the viewer. But as I look at this precious photograph taken, carried, developed, and digitized with care, how can I not mention that the sleeve of the adult covers the left eye of the baby they are holding? Such feedback rekindled in me the realization that when we look at an image, we see different worlds. Experienced alt text writers know this and have made their peace with it. I have not. And it strikes me that our immense perceptual subjectivity is central to the necessity of visual investigations. Recent news has only exacerbated this fact.

The most recent Israeli campaign in Gaza has proven to be fertile ground for visual investigations. Indeed, the military offensive fulfills two essential requirements for this kind of work: contested narratives and source materials.

This conflict is an inherently divisive one, with various parties espousing long-held and differing conceptions of the very nature of the history of the region, each producing opposing narratives. But that is not all. During the Hamas-led attack on October 7, 2023, the immediate Israeli military response in Israel, and the months-long onslaught in Gaza, there have been countless gun fights, artillery attacks, and, overwhelmingly, Israeli aerial strikes. Since October but continuing to this day, these strikes have caused mass civilian casualties on a near-daily basis. Airwars, a not-for-profit transparency watchdog that tracks, assesses, archives, and investigates civilian harm claims in conflict-affected nations, recorded more than 5,000 instances of civilian harm since October 7, in other words more than fifteen incidents per day.[1] Each of these incidents is ripe for a visual investigation. Many of these events are hotly contested, because both Israel and the military wing of Hamas, Al-Qassam brigades, have developed media branches. While the Hamas media arm mostly publishes lightly edited videos of clashes and successful operations, the Israeli military also regularly publishes annotated videos detailing the reasoning for an operation, using graphic design elements borrowed from visual investigations. More on this later.

The second requirement for visual investigations is also met: source material. There has been a torrent of audiovisual records for these debated events, consisting of photos, videos, live streams, and snapchats captured reflexively by people on the ground—Palestinians living day by day, capturing with their phones and sharing, when the internet connection suffices, what they see around them. Crucially, Palestinian journalists have also continuously risked their lives to document these events, actively walking toward strike sites and often reaching them before any form of medical help arrives on the scene.

However, in the past few weeks, images from Gaza have been sparser on my social media feed. In part this can be attributed to an extraordinarily lethal few months for journalists. The Committee to Protect Journalists reports that 108 journalists and media workers (two Israeli, three Lebanese, and 103 Palestinian) have been killed since October 7, in what amounts to the deadliest period for journalists since the organization began keeping track in 1992.[2] However, it can also be explained by the erosion of international interest in the conflict and shock at the violence depicted in its images.

At the time of writing, visual investigative teams in western news organizations have put their resources into the attempted assassination of former US president Donald J. Trump.

VISUAL INVESTIGATIONS AS COUNTER FORENSICS OR PHOTOJOURNALISM

As Israel's campaign in Gaza rages on, with accountability journalism and human rights investigations seeming to have little impact on the actions of Israeli military leaders, it bears asking what the field of visual investigations is good for. What work is it doing in the first place?

Eyal Weizman[3] and Thomas Keenan[4] conceptualize the heterogeneous set of truth practices, sometimes called visual investigations, forensic architecture, visual forensics, digital investigations, and every permutation thereof, as a bastardization of the state's forensics. These practices seek to turn the juridical gaze back onto the state or corporation in order to hold the powerful to account: a counter forensics. The field as a whole makes the case that certain acts, often hitherto not conceived as criminal in a juridical sense, are in fact crimes and did take place. On the technological level, in a seeming realization of late twentieth-century anarchist internet utopias, it is through the proliferation of social media that users have created a humanity-wide repository of audiovisual evidence, a world wide web of photos and videos rivaling the state's surveillance capabilities and providing us with the hard evidence to turn the forensic gaze back onto the state. Common sense would have us believe that these new digital investigative techniques emerged with this locker of public evidence. But what if these novel practices came about not from the proliferation of citizen journalism images, but from their failure—from the failure of the Twitter photo to force us to act by showing?

In his essay "Photographs of Agony," John Berger pinpoints how war photography, in this case from the Vietnam War, is meant to awaken concern.[5] The image should stir moral outrage in the viewer's mind, outrage that motivates political action to stop the causes of such agony. But, Berger argues, concern is not their effect. Not knowing where to assign responsibility, viewers end up accusing themselves, then "everybody and nobody," thus dispersing their shock and accusation. From photographs of the American Civil War, to the First World War, the Spanish Civil War, the evening news images of Vietnam, and the live footage of the Gulf War, to the livestreams of the twenty-first century, the goal of photojournalism to provoke moral outrage has erupted, bloomed, and dispersed. In today's daily images of conflict on social media, users simply scroll past the content warning screen. It is in this context that contemporary visual evidence practices should be understood.

Here, I will explore what placing visual investigations in the genealogy of photojournalism, rather than that of juridical forensics, can teach us about its necessity, argumentative goals, and limitations. I will argue that what visual investigations does is extend photography. The analyzed image, the image complex represented, is the next evolution of war photography. What it does is reinfuse shock into the image and extend our attention span in a world where photography has failed its promise.

THE LOOKING GLASS

One explanation for the birth of new digital truth practices is the loss of shock at the violent image. We don't see the violence, and we can't agree on what we see when we look at the image. So visual forensics breaks the image apart. It draws the violence on top of the image, like perspective lines on draft paper. When a felled wall, burned field, or torn body is incomprehensible to our mind, it diagrams the physical phenomena that led to such a result. It renders an incomprehensibly violent image the obvious result of well-known actions by well-known actors. It shows us how.

In order to do this, we, as practitioners, delve into very specific knowledge of weapons, geographies, anatomies, and audiovisual recording device functions. We say: "Ignore this artifact. It is a consequence of the specific physical documentation process. *This* is the specific feature you should care about." We use hyperspecificity as a tool to take control of debate: "This is the question that needs answering." For example, *The Washington Post* reconstructed the Israeli security forces' shooting of civilians in Nablus in 2023.[6] A video taken from above the scene was widely circulated online and showed the events. But it was through witness interviews, 3D-model-building documenting the security forces' point of view, and audio analysis counting the number of rounds shot (fourteen) that the visual forensics team was able to drive home the point: this event really happened. Argumentation through hyperspecificity: we force the core question of the debate to be a given by quantifying details of it.

TUNNEL VISION

Rightfully, a recurrent criticism of this kind of work is that it is marked by myopia or, in other words, tunnel vision. When the investigation pores over the details of a single case in a sea of other cases that also deserve attention, the criticism is fair. When the investigation clinically dissects the position of human bodies as though they were pieces on a chessboard, the criticism is fair. And yet this is what these new truth practices require. They are effective to the extent that the environment surrounding a contentious event—the digital representation of what may in fact be a victim's childhood home—is mapped into a cartesian system with x, y, and z coordinates, precise to a definite decimal number. It is this rigid technical framework that allows practitioners to make verifiable quantitative claims about the trajectory of a bullet. And it is that bullet trajectory that renders undeniable the culpability of the actor.

SELF-EVIDENT PROOF

The way visual investigations extends photography is by drawing onto the image. The reason it is effective is that it deploys technoscientific formal elements and vocabulary. Yet there is an inherent tension between the scientific method's open reproducibility and its authoritative expertise.

Examining the formal representation of visual investigations shows two things. The first is that it seeks to convince by showing. Distance radii, bullet trajectories, chemical heatmaps, and photograph capture locations are shown and derived on screen and graphically represent the investigation's findings. This form of open proof is part of the ethos of open source research work, a set of practices constitutive of visual forensics. The work is visually self-evident. An insinuated consequence of the field is that it is reproducible. This facet of forensics, that of reproducibility, is put forward as one of the tenets of the scientific method.

Secondly, the field of visual investigations also leverages general public trust in technical experts and scientists in another aspect: its graphic design. The graphic treatment of the grid, the primary-colored lines, the gray-scale modeling, and the use of rainbow colormaps mimics that of scientific diagrams. It seeks to assert technoscientific authority, implying that it goes through similar processes of peer review in order to convince the lay audience.

BLIND FAITH

Although anyone can reproduce the work, some of the techniques have become so advanced that they are indistinguishable from closed source work.

As visual investigations have become more widespread and ever more distant from the judicial and journalistic fields, the methodologies have continuously evolved. Beyond sheer experimentation, it feels like this evolution is driven by a chase. But what is the field chasing? Are we chasing the erosion of the power of, first of all, twentieth-century professional photojournalism; second, citizen journalism videos; and now, finally, the forensically analyzed image, causing us to look for further complex phenomena to analyze? As each medium loses its power to convey violence, we up the ante. Or are we chasing the visual literacy of the audience, knowing that as they grasp past methods, we can build in complexity? Either way, this evolution repositions visual forensics practitioners with more powerful, effective access to the truth. In doing so, it puts the audience symmetrically at a greater distance to truth, except through us. It becomes a sort of blind faith in the forensic shaman.

A synthetic third consideration is perhaps the most worrisome: are those two chases the same? Does increasing visual literacy yield an erosion of emotional potency? Is visual investigations only argumentatively potent when it plays at the limits of the audience's comprehension? Are we as practitioners content with this relationship of blind faith?

Cautionary examples abound. In her work on the Rodney King beating, Tory Jeffay lays out how the famous video was used during trial. Instead of highlighting what is self-evident in the footage at a high level—the LAPD officers beating an unarmed black man on the ground—the defense's police experts focused on how King's prone posture and micromovements, demonstrated in their frame-by-frame analysis, indicated his resistance and thus justified the use of force.[7] We see, then, that this "deconstructive gaze," the very same gaze deployed in new digital forensic techniques, has no claim to inherent accuracy, fairness, or truth.

An immediate solution is to submit such visual analysis to the same treatment. That same gaze can also be unleashed not only onto original citizen journalism footage, but onto visual analysis as well. In their assessment of visual evidence presented by the Israeli legal team at the ICJ, Forensic Architecture cross-examined diagramed footage and the claims they purport to prove, doing just that.[8]

CONCLUSION

Reading these new visual digital investigative techniques as the salvaging descendant of photojournalism helps us understand their value and limitations. Visual investigations' deconstructive gaze draws the unspoken violence in the conflict image. It leverages technoscientific authority to hold our attention on these contested events and helps us read a shared concept. But how should we deal with the contradictory positioning of self-evident open proofs and the necessity to trust the counter-forensic expert?

We find ourselves at an interesting moment in the development of the field, with the expanded use of audio analysis in the public sphere as part of visual investigations as well as in standalone efforts. One of the leading figures in this subfield,

Lawrence Abu Hamdan,[9] and the organization he leads, Earshot,[10] have been pioneering new forms of analysis. Perhaps even more importantly, they craft novel ways to communicate such analyses to lay audiences less familiar with waveforms than with orthographic maps. In a way, we are living through a rerun of the popularization of visual forensics methods, and can pay closer attention with a keen eye to the ways in which expertise is leveraged in the public forum. One clue comes from Earshot's recent investigation into attacks on media workers in Palestine.[11] In one of their visualizations (because even audio analysis is visualized for ease of communication) they labeled a waveform representing the audio recording of an explosion: flash, impact, muzzle blast—the usual moments that the audio latency analysis leverages to establish the distance of a munition source. But crucially, here the group also labeled other parts of the waveform: debris, glass, dust. This descriptive gesture, going beyond what is strictly necessary for analytical purposes and almost alt-texting the sound for a lay audience that can be described as audition-impaired in its lack of expertise at reading sounds in such a context, comes across as a slower, friendlier move to guide a beginner forum. Perhaps there is some benefit to having to explain across the media divide that grounds, at least in its current stage of normalization, public communication of such audio investigations.

As we continue to call for, produce, and watch visual investigations, the looking glass, tunnel vision, and blind faith will continue to present themselves. Keeping an eye out for these strategic moves and pitfalls helps us keep driving the field in a productive liberatory direction.

– July 2024, Beirut and Lenapehoking

1   https://airwars.org/conflict/israel-and-gaza-2023/.

2   https://cpj.org/2024/07/journalist-casualties-in-the-israel-gaza-conflict/.

3   https://www.sternberg-press.com/product/the-architecture-of-public-truth/.

4   https://www.greyroom.org/issues/55/39/counter-forensics-and-photography/.

5   John Berger, "Photographs of Agony," in *About Looking* (New York: Pantheon, 1980), 41–44.

6   https://www.washingtonpost.com/investigations/interactive/2023/palestine-shooting-nablus-videos.

7   "Manufactured Evidence," public talk by Tory Jeffay with respondent Kelli Moore, May 5, 2023, https://www.youtube.com/watch?v=FsauO6wH6Bc.

8   https://forensic-architecture.org/investigation/assessment-israeli-material-icj-jan-2024.

9   https://primaryinformation.org/product/live-audio-essays/.

10 https://earshot.ngo/.

11 https://earshot.ngo/investigations/5-attacks-on-journalists-in-palestine.

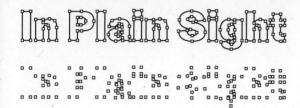

Remote Sensing and Land Dispossession in the West Bank

SITU Research, New York City, in collaboration with the Israeli human rights organization Yesh Din, Tel Aviv, attorney Michael Sfard, Tel Aviv, Adam Maloof and Ryan Manzuk of the Princeton University Department of Geoscience, New Jersey

2023-ongoing

SITU RESEARCH, SEE PAGE 27

Project participants: Gauri Bahuguna, Ramon Bieri, Bora Erden, and Brad Samuels

YESH DIN

Yesh Din is an Israeli human rights organization that documents, collects, and disseminates up-to-date information regarding systematic human rights violations in the Occupied Palestinian Territories.

Project participants: Firas Alami, Yair Foldes, Yonatan Kanonich, Alon Cohen Lifshitz, and Ziv Stahl

MICHAEL SFARD

Michael Sfard is an Israeli human rights lawyer and political activist specializing in international human rights law and the laws of war. He is the legal advisor of Yesh Din and has served as counsel in various cases with respect to the Israeli occupation in Israeli courts.

ADAM MALOOF

Adam Maloof, Professor of Geoscience, Princeton University

RYAN MANZUK

Ryan Manzuk, PhD candidate, Department of Geoscience, Princeton University

In June 1967, following the conclusion of the '67 war, Israel captured the Golan Heights from Syria, the West Bank including East Jerusalem from Jordan, and the Gaza Strip and the Sinai Peninsula from Egypt. In November of that same year, as part of an effort to create a roadmap for an enduring peace in the region, the United Nations Security Council passed Resolution 242. Among its many points, this resolution called for the "withdrawal of Israeli armed forces from territories occupied in recent conflict" and the "termination of all claims or states of belligerency and respect for and acknowledgment of the sovereignty, territorial integrity and political independence of every State in the area and their right to live in peace within secure and recognized boundaries free from threats or acts of force."[1]

Following the adoption of Resolution 242, what began as a seizure of land in wartime became an enduring occupation, and in the months and years that followed, Israeli settlements began to proliferate across the West Bank and continued to pick up momentum over the ensuing decades. At the present moment this includes 146 authorized settlements and 205 unauthorized outposts (settlements that were built without the proper Israeli official authorizations) as well as roads, industrial zones, nature reserves, and more.

Today, with Palestinian communities surrounded by Israeli settler developments and subject to separate and repressive laws, the regime in the West Bank can be described as one which provides distinct and unequal legal rights to Jewish Israelis and Palestinians, respectively. The fact that the law in the West Bank effectively functions as a two-tiered system of rules, rights, and protections—one modern, generated by an elected legislator and affording to Israelis all the rights and protections usually given to citizens in a liberal democracy, the other military and draconian, applying to Palestinians—has been one of several reasons for allegations that Israel has been committing the crime of apartheid. Apartheid, which is classified as a crime against humanity, was defined in both the 1973 International Convention on the Suppression and Punishment of the Crime of Apartheid[2] and the 1998 Rome Statute of the International

Study area for agricultural access restrictions in and near the seam zone in the northeastern region of the occupied West Bank. Test group (white) and control group (black) tiles are used to track changes in the NDVI over time at specific sites containing olive orchards. The NDVI change image shown here was derived from 2023 Landsat 8 satellite imagery, courtesy of the U.S. Geological Survey. The black line indicates the route of the separation barrier sourced from unaltered, 2018 geospatial data from OCHA.

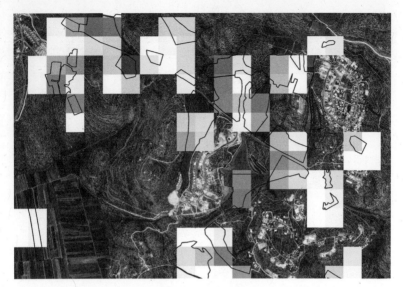

Sample collection of assets used in analyzing Israeli settler agricultural expansion in the central region of the occupied West Bank. High-resolution satellite imagery taken on August 19, 2023, at 50 cm resolution is overlaid with a NDVI image at 150 m resolution derived from 2021 Landsat satellite imagery, courtesy of the U.S. Geological Survey. Each NDVI pixel is the averaged NDVI values of a 5×5 pixel tile from the 2021 Landsat image. Polygons indicate vineyards and orchards targeted in the analysis. High-resolution satellite image © CNES (2023), Distribution AIRBUS DS.

Haroun Kahla, a Palestinian farmer and member of the displaced community of Wadi al-Seeq, points to his agricultural land that he is unable to access and speaks about his experience of being forcibly displaced. By providing a personal account of events, locations, and contextual information, testimony from Mr. Kahla and others becomes an important source of ground-truthing data for the remote sensing analyses.

Criminal Court.[3] Albeit with slightly different wording, both treatises generally frame apartheid in the same terms, with the latter defining it as inhumane acts of a character similar to other crimes against humanity "committed in the context of an institutionalized regime of systematic oppression and domination by one racial group over any other racial group or groups and committed with the intention of maintaining that regime." Systematic oppression and domination are thus a key component of the crime, which usually translates to a reality of chronic supremacy of the dominant group over the inferior group in rights and resources.

This project is seeking to document and analyze the changes in land use and land possession in the West Bank. Given that the Israeli-Palestinian conflict is a territorial one, it is the team's aim to examine whether the systematic discrimination has a spatial representation and whether remote sensing over space and time shows patterns of disinheritance in relation to lands in the West Bank.

To be considered a crime against humanity under international law, a violation must be widespread or systematic and directed against the civilian population. Hence, demonstrating that such violation resulted in harms that are demonstrably widespread or systematic has probative value regarding this element of the crime. It is within this framing that the joint project has assembled a body of evidence that speaks to the spatial and temporal manifestation of the occupation that—the project participants believe—may be consistent with the crime of apartheid. While there are many potential examples of these manifestations, this project specifically analyzes several instances of forced displacement, land dispossession, physical violence, and denial of access to farmland, which serve as case studies and provide a methodology that can and hopefully will be used in numerous other instances. Although there has long been witness testimony recounting these conditions—much of it coming from Palestinian residents of the West Bank—by recounting these conditions, there has been a dearth of quantitative analysis on this issue. The goal of this project is to assemble a case file that examines the oppression and domination element of the crime of apartheid, through its particular manifestation in the form of denial of access to and use of lands, and to do so through evidence that provides *both* a strong testimonial *and* scientific evidentiary base. While human rights organizations such as Yesh Din, Human Rights Watch, and Amnesty International have all produced seminal reports regarding their findings of apartheid in the Occupied Palestinian Territory, it is the team's understanding that this project may be the first time an effort has been made to assemble a body of quantitative evidence that addresses one feature of the crime of apartheid in the context of the West Bank.

This work, a collaboration between Israeli human rights organization Yesh Din, attorney Michael Sfard, SITU Research, and Princeton University's Department of Geoscience, focuses on three distinct violations that can be understood as manifestations of an apartheid regime: Israeli settler dispossession of agricultural Palestinian land, forced displacement of Palestinian communities, and limitation or restriction of access to Palestinian agricultural land in the Seam Zone.[4] These investigative priorities are pursued through the analysis of a range of satellite and aerial imagery in relation to on-site documentation and through witness testimony. The analysis focuses on evaluating the types of relevant land cover change that can be viewed from space. A key component of this work is monitoring changes in land use, particularly in agriculture. One indicator of this change is the transition from olive groves, in an area typically tended to by Palestinian farmers, to grape vineyards, in an area typically tended to by Israeli settlers. Understanding when the former has changed into the latter is often a good proxy for documenting a key part of certain instances of land dispossession.

With a focus on documenting agricultural changes such as these, the team applied a novel method to detect olive-orchard and grape-vineyard land use through multispectral analysis of Landsat data, a US space agency satellite initiative established in 1972. While most morphological features of vegetation and

Abdelkarim Shamasneh, a Palestinian farmer from the town of Nabi Elias, points to his olive orchards and agricultural land that lie beyond the separation barrier in the seam zone. Mr. Shamasneh has been unable to access this land or harvest his olives regularly in this area for the last seven to eight years. He has been completely prohibited from this land for the last three years.

An olive branch with olives, ca. 1900–1920. Olive trees have been cultivated in the area now called the occupied West Bank for millennia.

Remote Sensing and Land Dispossession in the West Bank

crops cannot be identified in Landsat's thirty meter pixel resolution, a targeted time series Normalized Difference Vegetation Index (NDVI) analysis, combined with a calibration of seasonal patterns expected of differing agricultural practices, allows the researchers to detect and time-stamp changes to agricultural land use in this region and compare it to witness testimony. This method, while first applied to a selection of currently accessible sites, has been developed for broad application across the West Bank with the goal of determining the geographic and temporal extent of these violations.

On July 19, 2024, in a significant development that occurred during the course of work on this project, the International Court of Justice issued an Advisory Opinion that declared the Israeli occupation of Palestinian Territory, including the West Bank, unlawful. As an authoritative opinion issued by the world's highest court on matters of international law, this ruling paves the way for potential future litigation across multiple jurisdictions. This work of this project and the methods developed along with it will be made available to legal teams as both advocacy and litigation is pursued in the coming months and years.

1   United Nations Security Council (1967) Resolution 242, 22 November 1967, S/RES/242, https://peacemaker.un.org/sites/peacemaker.un.org/files/SCRes242%281967%29.pdf.

2   International Convention on Suppression and Punishment of the Crime of Apartheid, Nov 30, 1973, Exec. Doc.(A/C.3/L.1871), https://legal.un.org/avl/pdf/ha/cspca/cspca_ph_e.pdf.

3   Rome Statute of the International Criminal Court, 1998, UN Doc. A/CONF.183/9, 2187 UNTS 90, entered into force July 1, 2002 ("Rome Statute"), art. 7, https://www.icc-cpi.int/resourcelibrary/documents/rs-eng.pdf.

4   The Seam Zone is the area between the so-called Green Line (the 1949 Armistice border) and the separation barrier erected by Israel. The Seam Zone is heavily controlled legally and militarily. It is considered a "closed area" that Palestinians are only allowed to enter with special permits. These permits are necessary to gain access to their land, work, or other essential services.

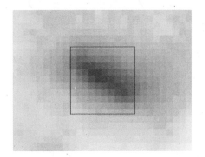 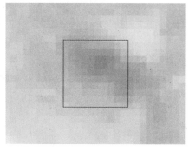

This 3 meter resolution satellite image from Planet Labs, taken on June 16, 2023, isolates blue light from the image to highlight a building in dark blue pixels. This building was a school for children from the displaced communities of Ras al-Tin and al-Qaboun. PlanetScope satellite image © 2023, Planet Labs PBC.

This 3 meter resolution satellite image from Planet Labs taken on July 31, 2024, also utilizing blue light, shows a dramatic reduction in the dark-blue pixels of the building. This change is consistent with a similar analysis at a documented school demolition site in the nearby community of Ein Samiya, indicating that the Ras al-Tin school was likely demolished at some point between mid-June 2023 and July 2024. PlanetScope satellite image © 2024, Planet Labs PBC.

The interviews with the Palestinian farmers seen in the photographs were conducted by Firas Alami, Head of Field Department, Yesh Din, and Muner Qaddus, Field Researcher, Yesh Din.

Scan the QR code to access a film on the methodology of the project.

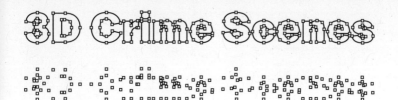

Forensic Reconstruction and Visualization

Ralf Breker

RALF BREKER

Ralf Breker is head of the Forensic Media Technology Department at the Bavarian State Office of Criminal Investigation. He studied geomedia technology at the Hochschule München – University of Applied Sciences and has worked at the Forensic Institute of the Bavarian State Office of Criminal Investigation since 2009. Since the beginning of his career, he has served as an advisor and prepares expert reports for the police, the public prosecutor's office, the courts, and the Bavarian State Ministry of the Interior. In 2015, he was also appointed head of Department 212 – Forensic Media Technology. Among his projects were the historical 3D reconstructions of the Auschwitz-Birkenau concentration camp and the attack on the Oktoberfest on September 26, 1980.

In the year 2009, Peter Dathe, then President of the Bavarian State Office of Criminal Investigation (BLKA), decided on the procurement of surveying instruments for 3D visualization of crime scenes. These instruments—a terrestrial laser scanner (TLS)[1] for large-scale crime scenes and a stripe light scanner[2] for small items and evidence objects—were assigned to forensics or, more specifically, to the subject area of 212 forensic media technology. Since then, capital offenses, traces, and evidence objects in Bavaria have been captured three-dimensionally.

THREE-DIMENSIONAL FORENSICS

Capturing crime scenes with the help of TLS changed the forensic work of the BLKA's subject area 212 fundamentally: instead of using pictures and videos with distorted perspectives for documentation purposes only, the 3D point clouds resulting from the scan are used for further forensic investigations, thus preserving the crime scenes in three dimensions. The new forensic possibilities are also valuable for evaluating evidence: investigators can now visualize trajectories (spatial curves) of blood spatter and their focal points in the 3D scene, for example. Profile traces, made visible through Luminol,[3] can be integrated into the digital model without distortion, and visual axes of witnesses and suspects can be inserted in a mathematically correct way. → FIG. 1 Based on surveillance videos and 3D scans, the BLKA can now even determine the height of perpetrators depicted in video footage, and the models can also be used to check the plausibility of complex crime sequences.

On a small scale, completely new areas of application have been opened up in the preservation of traces and evidence since the use of strip light scanners began. For example, possible traces of injury on the body of harmed people—caused by objects or kicks to the head—can be precisely measured and compared with possible sources of the traces. In addition to the 3D surface images of the traces of injury, it is posisble to take computer tomography (CT) imagery[4] of the injured areas and combine it with data from the structured light scanner. Bone defects caused by blunt force can be transferred to the model

Figure 1. Projected photo with fluorescent luminol in the scan

3D Crime Scenes: Forensic Reconstruction and Visualization

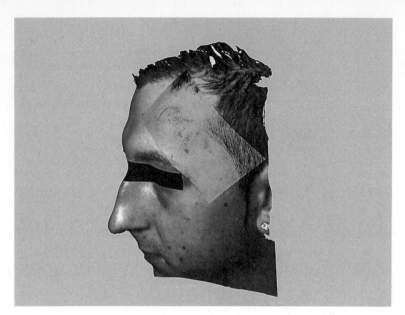

Figure 2.   Reconstruction of an injury pattern

and matched with the superficial 3D data. Based on accurate 3D structured-light scans, one is able to reconstruct injury patterns even years after a crime. Provided that the trace pattern was photographed at the time, the injured topography—for example, on the head—can be scanned and the photo projected onto the 3D surface of the head based on matching features between the photo and the scan, allowing the trace to be analyzed. → FIG. 2

DIGITAL RECONSTRUCTION OF HISTORICAL CRIME SCENES

Since their procurement, 3D technologies have become an indispensable part of police work and are also establishing themselves in criminal proceedings in court. Four years after their introduction at the BLKA, the Department 212 Forensic Media Technology was commissioned to reconstruct the Auschwitz-Birkenau concentration camp. As part of the nationwide investigation into former guards from the Schutzstaffel (SS) under National Socialism in Germany, a 3D model of the concentration camp was to be created that for use in court. This enabled investigators to reconstruct the lines of sight of the SS guards— for example, the view from a watchtower toward the crematoria.

The digital, three-dimensional reconstruction of one of the largest crime scenes in history was a major challenge for the department because of the area's spatial extent and the research work required. First, an inventory had to be carried out on the site. Preserved buildings, such as barracks, saunas, and watchtowers, could be recorded three-dimensionally using a laser scanner. Buildings that no longer existed, such as the crematoria, had to be extensively remodeled[5] based on the construction plans from Auschwitz.

For the 3D reconstruction of the Auschwitz-Birkenau concentration camp, Department 212 also used virtual reality (VR) technology for the first time: investigators and prosecutors were not only able to view the model on a monitor but also to "immerse" themselves in the 3D scene using VR headsets. This gave the viewers an objective impression of the camp. The question mentioned above about the lines of sight of the SS guards could be answered satisfactorily with the help of this new technology. The resulting 3D model of the camp was eventually used in the trial against the former SS guard Reinhold Hanning, after the SS member Johann Breyer, in whose trial the model was also to have been used, died before being deported from the United States. → FIG. 3

Virtual reality has also been employed in the reconstruction of another historic case: the Oktoberfest attack on September 26, 1980. When the special commission "Soko 26 September" resumed its investigations in 2014, the site of the attack on the Theresienwiese in Munich was reconstructed based on laser scans, digital terrain models, and orthographic photos—analogous to the Auschwitz reconstruction. In addition, a large number of photos of the attack site, taken by the police, rescue services, and the press, were made available to Department 212. Based on this data, an exact and clear 3D/VR model could be created on the basis of which various investigations were carried out.

In subsequent years, the establishment of virtual realities for the visualization of 3D laser scan data was used more and more frequently, so the department developed the first "VR viewer," that is, an application for playing VR data, based on a game engine[6] called Unity. Initial experiences with the application demonstrated the diverse possible applications of the technology for virtual documentation, reconstruction, and analysis of crime scenes. In 2019, it was finally decided to develop an even more innovative and complex VR application for forensic media technology: the "Holodeck" became the flagship project of the Bavarian police. After a total development time of four years, it was presented to the public on June 6, 2023, at a press conference.[7]

THE HOLODECK

The 70-square-meter room at the BLKA's Munich location is divided into a spectator area and an application area. Equipped

Figure 3. Reconstruction of the Auschwitz-Birkenau concentration camp

Figure 4. The Holodeck

Figure 5. Multiuser scene with spectators and moderator

with the latest high-end technology from the field of digital media technologies, digitized crime scenes can be visualized as VR content in the Holodeck based on laser scans and photogrammetry. → FIG. 4 However, the Holodeck is by no means a pure visualization platform. Rather, it serves investigators, forensics, and the public prosecutor's office through the availability of a variety of tools for analysis, documentation, and reconstruction for to dealing with specific questions at the virtual crime scene. To ensure constructive virtual crime scene work, appropriate technical framework conditions had to be created and various functions implemented.

The Holodeck is a multiuser application, enabling up to one hundred users to participate in a meeting simultaneously. Regardless of location, they are able to interact, exchange data, and communicate with other participants in virtual locations. Every action of a user is visibly replicated for all other participants in the network. → FIG. 5 This specially developed role concept enables a controlled use of the technology in multiuser mode:

In the role of the viewer, the user's hands are visualized in virtual reality using "hand tracking." With the virtual hands, users can operate a display that allows them to independently navigate through a 3D scene, grasp objects, and use documentation tools. Users in the moderator role are enabled by special tools to guide the audience, for example, to gather audience members behind them or to direct people to another area of the crime scene. In the specific application, this role can be taken on by the public prosecutor, investigators, or forensic units. The standard role is that of the active user, who has access to the software's entire range of reconstruction, documentation, and analysis tools. The Holodeck's user role concept enables the implementation of innovative, interactive presentations. In addition, people who have not been to the real crime scene can be introduced to the virtual crime scene by moderators. In addition, the ease of use of the functions in spectator mode ensures that even nontechnical people have full access to VR scenarios.

Active users are visualized as ultra-realistic, user-identical avatars: with the help of a photogrammetric full-body scanner, movements of active users in the Holodeck can be transferred to the avatar in real time. → FIG. 6 The full-body scanner is equipped with seventy cameras. With a mouse click, all cameras are triggered simultaneously and the seventy resulting individual images are calculated to form a 3D avatar. This is then embedded as a virtual skeleton in the Unreal game engine. The recording and transfer of movements to the avatar takes place in the so-called motion capture system.[8] By creating digital copies of the users, a personified presence is created in the virtual world. Tracking technologies extend the classic digital communication channels to include body language, creating an immersive social presence for the participants. This has enormous potential in terms of communication between police officers, but also when questioning suspects or witnesses in virtual reality. The software developed also supports various media platforms and is therefore not spatially limited to the Holodeck. A VR headset is not necessary; in network or stand-alone mode, access to 3D scenarios is also possible with a classic PC or mobile device.

Due to their design and the integration of appropriate real-time functions and tools, the Holodeck and its software are much more than just an application for visualizing VR content. Rather, it represents an innovative, virtual working environment for investigators, experts, and prosecutors and is thus the first real police VR laboratory in the Federal Republic of Germany. The Holodeck forms the basis for a virtual, criminalistic platform that enables continuous, modular construction. This platform is by no means limited to forensic use to support investigations but can be expanded at any time to other areas of operation of the (Bavarian) police. In the next development step, the Holodeck software will be equipped with AI functionalities that will enable a transformation of the 3D models into real digital twins in the medium term. At the end of this text, let me remind you: the history of 3D visualization at the BLKA began just fifteen years ago with the acquisition of 3D surveying instruments ...

Figure 6. Member of the forensic media technology team in the full-body scanner

1. A terrestrial laser scanner (TLS) generates up to 50 million measurement points with an accuracy in the millimeter range. The resulting scans are displayed in grayscale: the more the emitted laser beam is reflected on a surface, the brighter the measurement point appears in the visualization; the weaker the reflection, the darker it is. By taking 360-degree panoramic photographs, it is also possible to display the metrologically precise and dense 3D grayscale point clouds in true colors.

2. The 3D stripe light scanner works with submillimeter accuracy and is used, for example, to record profile tracks. When photographing tracks on flat surfaces without 3D technology, it is essential to ensure that the photo is parallel to the plane in order to keep perspective distortion as low as possible. If this recording configuration deviates even slightly, then the track photo quickly shows distortions in the centimeter range—for a profile track on the ground, this corresponds to one or two shoe sizes. In addition, an image scale must always be set in the plane of the track. Precise evaluations of tracks on curved, that is, non-flat surfaces are difficult or impossible without the use of 3D technologies: if a curved 3D surface is depicted on a two-dimensional plane, the image scale of every single pixel changes. For this reason, a natural object can only be shown with distortion in a photo. With the 3D stripe light scanner, traces on curved surfaces can also be recorded and evaluated true to scale.

3. In forensics, luminol is used to search for traces to detect even the smallest amounts of blood. When it reacts with oxidizing agents such as hydrogen peroxide, a bluish light is released. This light can be made visible in a darkened room and makes it possible to detect traces of blood that would not be visible to the naked eye.

4. Computer tomography (CT for short) is a special 3D X-ray examination that creates cross-sectional images of the body. These cross-sectional images contain 3D information that can be calculated into accurate 3D models.

5. Serving as the basis for the reconstruction are digital terrain models (DTM), which are 3D topographies of the area without buildings or vegetation. A high-resolution, distortion-free, orthographic photo of the area was projected onto this model. Both the remodeled 3D models and those generated by the laser scanner were finally able to be precisely integrated into the terrain data provided by the surveying office.

6. "Engine" describes a framework system that provides all the building blocks needed to develop a game for a specific platform. The use of engines has become established beyond the gaming scene, but most of these "building blocks" are provided by game developers.

7. The press conference to present the Holodeck on June 6, 2023, was chaired by Joachim Herrmann, Bavarian Minister of State of the Interior, for Sport and Integration, Judith Gerlach, then Bavarian Minister of State for Digital Affairs, and Harald Pickert, then President of the Bavarian State Criminal Police Office.

8. With the help of sixteen high-precision infrared measuring cameras, so-called clusters on the hands, feet, back, and head of the active users are tracked, thereby determining their position in space. Eye-tracking also records pupil movements and eyelids, and face-tracking transfers facial expressions to the avatar.

The Sound of Bullets

Investigating the Killing of Colombian Journalist Abelardo Liz

Bellingcat, Amsterdam, in collaboration with Cerosetenta, Bogotá

2023

BELLINGCAT

Bellingcat is an independent investigative collective composed of researchers, investigators, and citizen journalists united by their passion for open source research. The collective operates with over thirty staff members and contributors from more than twenty countries. Established in 2014, Bellingcat has been at the forefront of using open source methods to investigate significant public interest issues such as the shooting down of flight MH17 over eastern Ukraine, police violence in Colombia, and the illegal wildlife trade in the United Arab Emirates. Their work is frequently referenced by international media and cited by courts and investigative missions.

Bellingcat is known for designing and sharing verifiable methods of ethical digital investigation. They publish guides to open source research methods and provide tailored training sessions for journalists, human rights activists, and the general public. This helps broaden the scope and application of open source research.

Project participants: Lucy Swinnen, Carlos Gonzales, Galen Reich, and Charlotte Maher

CEROSETENTA

Cerosetenta is an independent digital media platform founded at the Center for Journalism Studies (CEPER) of the Universidad de los Andes. This outlet bridges the gap between academic research and journalistic practice, striving to cultivate journalism that is free, innovative, and committed to addressing contemporary issues. Combining rigorous academic methods with journalistic storytelling, Cerosetenta covers national news and explores critical issues relevant to the twenty-first century.

Project participants: María Angélica Riascos Sierra, Natalia Arenas, Diego Forero, and Tania Tapia

On August 13, 2020, Indigenous Colombian journalist Abelardo Liz was fatally shot while filming a confrontation between Colombian army soldiers and Indigenous Nasa protesters at a land rights demonstration on a hacienda, a large estate, about five hundred kilometers southwest of the capital city of Bogotá. Despite large quantities of publicly available evidence about the shooting, no one has been held accountable for his death.

Investigative journalists at the Colombian media outlet Cerosetenta approached open source investigators at Bellingcat to help sift through the evidence from the shooting, including footage recorded by Abelardo Liz himself capturing the exact moment he was shot. This collaboration aimed to expose inconsistencies in the Colombian army's account of events.

The Indigenous Nasa people have been engaging in what they call "Liberación de la Madre Tierra," a process by which they are occupying territory they say has been taken away from them since Spanish colonization. Land in the Cauca region has historically been concentrated in the hands of agribusinesses, resulting in the displacement of the Nasa people to less fertile areas, thereby limiting their ability to sustain themselves.

According to a report in the journal *Revista Estudios Socio-Jurídicos,* this displacement has pushed the Nasa to employ land occupation tactics that stretch legal boundaries, creating tensions in the region. In addition, the Nasa community has been affected by territorial conflicts between drug trafficking cartels, Revolutionary Armed Forces of Colombia (FARC) dissidents, the Colombian military, police, and other armed groups. These conflicts have resulted in the deaths of Nasa community members.

Prior to this case, Bellingcat investigated the fatal shooting of Palestinian journalist Shireen Abu Akleh in 2022. Faced in this instance with a more complex shooting, they assumed the audio recordings of the gunshots would provide vital clues as to where the fatal shots had come from. A key part of the investigation therefore involves audio analysis. The investigators

Still images showing soldiers from Aguila 1 firing gunshots into the ground. In disciplinary investigations they denied having fired dissuasive shots.

A photogrammetry model showing the location of soldiers and the community seconds before the shooting started.

synchronized the sound patterns created by dozens of gun-shots recorded by different video cameras spread across a one-kilometer radius on the hacienda. Audio forensic experts Dr. Robert Maher and Steven D. Beck then analyzed the sounds of the supersonic bullets from sixteen videos to identify in detail how the shooting unfolded.

The findings assembled by Bellingcat and Cerosetenta contradict the Colombian army's version of events as well as several key claims made by soldiers in sworn testimonies about the shooting. The complex sound analysis found that soldiers appear to have started the shooting and that they fired their weapons into the ground at close range to civilians. Furthermore, the researchers found no evidence that the army came under fire from the mountains, contradicting the army's claims.

Concerning the fatal shot that killed Liz, the analysis showed that it appears to have come from an area where Colombian soldiers and other security forces were located. The bullet found in Liz's body was consistent with the type of bullets and weapons carried by the soldiers that day.

An immersive audio installation developed in 2024 for the Architecture Museum of the Technical University of Munich aims to recreate the events of August 13, 2020, and explains the concepts and techniques used in the analysis. It seeks to share details of the sound analysis in the hope that it will empower researchers, human rights activists, journalists, and open source investigators to carry out this work.

In response to the team's publication, four United Nations Special Rapporteurs wrote to the Colombian government in January 2024, calling for an urgent review of the case. They expressed concern at the excessive use of force by soldiers and their apparent impunity. Bellingcat and Cerosetenta's journalistic piece documenting the investigation process and findings was recognized as Runner-Up in the Innovation category at the European Press Prize in 2024.

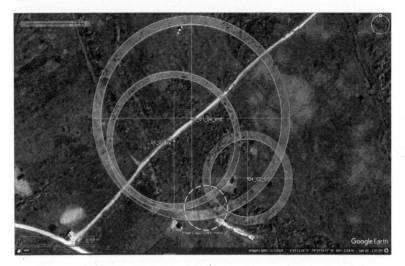

Full circles indicate the approximate range of distance to a potential shooter; dashed circle indicates where the full circles meet, indicating location of a possible shooter. However, there is some uncertainty due to the lack of ballistic data, including the speed and trajectory of the bullets. The location is an estimate.
Sources: Dr. Robert Maher, Google Earth Pro CNES-Airbus.

Scan the QR code for additional information and exhibition views of the installation at the Architecture Museum of the Technical University of Munich in 2024–25.

Documenting the Death Flights

SITU Research, New York City, in collaboration with Centro Prodh, Mexico City, and Alicia de los Ríos Merino

2023–24

SITU RESEARCH, SEE PAGE 27

Project participants: Gauri Bahuguna, Ramon Bieri, Martina Duque Gonzalez, Evan Grothjan, Sam Rabiyah, Brad Samuels, and Candice Strongwater

MIGUEL AGUSTÍN PRO JUÁREZ HUMAN RIGHTS CENTER

The Miguel Agustín Pro Juárez Human Rights Center (Centro Prodh) is a leading human rights organization in Mexico. Founded in 1988 by the Society of Jesus, the center works hand in hand with victims of some of Mexico's most emblematic cases of human rights abuses in their quest for truth and justice. With the support of Centro Prodh's integral legal defense and advocacy strategies, victims and collectives have exposed human rights abuses, fought impunity, and held perpetrators accountable at the national and international level.

ALICIA DE LOS RÍOS MERINO

Alicia de los Ríos Merino is a historian and lecturer in the Faculty of Arts at the Autonomous University of Chihuahua. As an attorney and family member of a person who disappeared in the context of the counterinsurgency, she is actively engaged in the investigations and truth efforts related to grave human rights violations committed during the period of the so-called "Dirty War" atrocities. Alicia carries the same name as her disappeared mother, Alicia de los Ríos Merino, who was an active member of the Liga Comunista 23 de Septiembre, an urban guerrilla group in Mexico during the 1970s. In January 1978, her mother was forcibly disappeared by the Brigada Blanca, a counterinsurgency unit made up of military personnel and agents from the Federal Security Directorate (DFS).

From the late 1960s to the early 1980s, the Mexican government intensified its brutal campaign against political dissidents in what is known as *la guerra sucia,* the "Dirty War." Extrajudicial executions, disappearances, torture, and other serious human rights violations became systematic practices to eliminate individuals perceived as threats. Due to the persistent efforts of victim-led justice organizations, in 2021 former Mexican president Andrés Manuel López Obrador (2018–24) signed an executive order establishing a Truth Commission to investigate this period. Despite expectations raised by the initiative, the investigation faced many obstacles, including lack of access to military records, which inhibited its ability to deliver on its mandate.

As a pathway to truth, reconciliation, and clarifying the historical record, Centro Prodh, a leading human rights organization based in Mexico City, worked with SITU Research to analyze and reconstruct one of the state's most clandestine programs of enforced disappearances: the so-called "death flights." These consisted of secret illegal operations in which political prisoners were tortured, killed, and then thrown into the sea from military aircrafts. This method, reminiscent of practices in Argentina, Uruguay, and Chile, was used by the Mexican military to leave no trace of their victims' whereabouts. To date, the identities of the victims remain unknown. However, this project highlights the story of one of many victims of enforced disappearances during this period: Alicia de los Ríos Merlno, an educator and young insurgent, whose final known whereabouts lead to the air base from where the death flights program was carried out.

The fourteen-minute video presents one of the first assemblages of visual evidence showing the highly organized program of disappearances conducted by key military officials in Guerrero, Mexico. This work weaves together both open and closed source research, a digital 3D site model reconstructed from archival materials, high resolution-declassified spy satellite imagery, and official records from a 2002 military investigation. A broad range of assets were analyzed, including

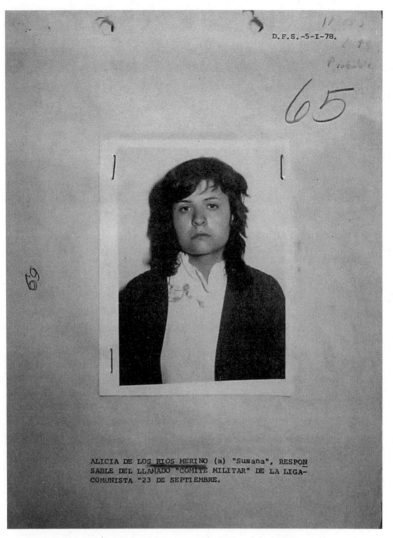

Arrest record of Alicia de los Ríos Merino from January 1978. captured by the Dirección Federal de Seguridad (D.F.S.). The document represents one of the last official records of her whereabouts.

Documenting the Death Flights

Declassified HEXAGON KH-9 reconnaissance satellite image shows parts of Guerrero, Mexico, from 1975. The image was used by researchers to determine the location of the Pie de la Cuesta Air Force Base.

3D site model reconstruction incorporates detainee photographs used in the investigation "The Death Flights."

Scan the QR code for additional information and visual material.

138   Case Study

documents from the National Security Archives, family photographs of Alicia de los Ríos Merino, one of the possible victims of the death flights, and unexpected Hollywood film footage that aided in the reconstruction of the Pie de la Cuesta Air Force Base, one of the primary crime scenes.

Widely circulated in Mexico, the video's call to action demands the release of the full scope of the military's archives in order to uncover additional aspects of the truth about this dark period of Mexican history.

Initiating the Counter Evidentiary Network

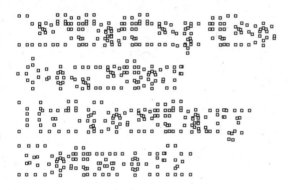

Toward a "Solidarity-Based" Mode of Open Source Investigation

Patrick Brian Smith

PATRICK BRIAN SMITH

Patrick Brian Smith is a University Fellow in the School of Arts, Media and Creative Technology at the University of Salford. He completed his PhD at Concordia University in 2020 and was previously a British Academy Postdoctoral Fellow at the University of Warwick. He is currently working on a project entitled "Counter Evidentiary Futures." His research interests include documentary theory and practice, spatial and political theory, forensic media, and human rights media activism. His book *Spatial Violence and the Documentary Image* was published with Legenda/MHRA in 2024. He is the co-convener of the BAFTSS Documentary SIG and a member-at-large for the SCMS Media, Science, and Technology Studies SIG. His work has been published in journals such as *JCMS, Discourse, Media, Culture & Society,* and NECSUS.

Open source investigation (OSI) is arguably at an inflection point. OSI practices have been widely heralded as expanding "platforms for political engagement," creating "new democratic practices to campaign, generate evidence, and sustain alternative stories for humanitarianism and activism,"[1] while also allowing "ordinary people . . . [to] influence international fact-finding processes."[2] OSI is increasingly regarded as a field that allows for more egalitarian approaches to investigating human rights violations and broader forms of corporate and political violence. With investigations being carried out at far removes from the physical sites in question—using data gleaned from covert sources as well as publicly available information—there is arguably a leveling of the investigative field, with practices that were previously the exclusive purview of specialist investigators or field journalists being opened up to anyone with an internet connection and some basic digital sleuthing skills (geo-location, chronolocation, remote sensing, audio analysis, and pattern analysis, among others). These narratives of democratization and liberation have been the key drivers behind OSI's rapid, interdisciplinary expansion across the fields of investigative journalism, human rights law, and new media practice.

At the same time, voices in the field have highlighted a range of ethical and epistemological tensions that are emerging within OSI as it is slowly codified and solidified as a set of methods and practices. For example, Nishat Awan argues that while such forms of "digital witnessing" enhance our ability to observe distant places, they also risk causing subaltern and racialized subjects to become less visible. More precisely, Awan cautions that OSI practices might mistakenly identify the act of making things visible as an "emancipatory act in itself," thereby suppressing subaltern, embodied experiences of violence.[3] Relatedly, Libby McAvoy argues that sharp divisions are being reinforced between "content-creators" and "content-analyzers" within the OSI field. For her, when OSI investigators examine materials showing violent and traumatic events, it is primarily the investigators who shape—and ultimately take ownership—of the analysis and narrative, rather than those individuals who captured, or featured in, the footage.[4] Thus, the agency of those who are materially affected by such forms of harm and violence is suppressed; they are often sidelined within the investigatory process.

McAvoy is a legal advisor at Mnemonic, an NGO dedicated to archiving, investigating, and memorializing digital information documenting human rights violations and international crimes. In 2021, she published a short piece through *Open Global Rights* entitled "Centering the 'source' in open source investigation." Here, she argued that the OSI field is divided by a binary of its own making, separating those who do the analytical and investigatory work from the "content-creators," who are often the ones closest to the documented harms. This process "weakens, ignores, and even severs the possibility of solidarity across a fabricated content-creator/content-analyzer divide."[5] For her, such divisions must be actively resisted. This resistance is essential because outsider researchers risk creating an echo chamber that mirrors, contributes to, and entrenches the harms already present in the "documentation-to-justice pipeline."[6] Instead, organizations should blend digital methods with avowedly "solidarity-based" practices to avoid undermining justice efforts and marginalizing those affected communities who are the subjects of investigations.[7] Consequently, OSI practices should support, not replace, local accountability efforts, which can also help to bridge the content-creator/content-analyzer divide. This solidarity-based approach should involve "deliberate, negotiated, genuine, transnational collaboration between advocates in the Global North and the Global South. It requires creating a common framework . . . that redistributes and balances burdens and benefits."[8]

I open here by mapping these various positions, not only to highlight the emerging ethical and epistemological tensions within the OSI field, but also to foreground the stakes of the Counter Evidentiary Network (CEN), a new research initiative in the School of Arts, Media and Creative Technology at the University of Salford. This interdisciplinary and collaborative network aims to foster dialogue, critical reflection, and knowledge exchange between various practice- and research-based open source investigation groups and individuals who are involved in exposing human rights violations and other forms of corporate and political violence. The CEN aims to explore and develop the multifarious democratic and liberatory potentialities of OSI, as identified by Gutiérrez, McDermott, Koenig, and Murray, among others. At the same time, the network also aims to concretely confront the thorny ethical and epistemological issues that have been identified by the likes of Awan and McAvoy.

The network is built around two primary components. The first aims to map how the OSI field currently operates, identifying knowledge and resource gaps as well as fostering space for further interconnection, collaboration, and expertise sharing. The OSI field is rapidly expanding and shifting in its disciplinary groundings. We have seen increased adoption of OSI methods across a broad range of adjacent fields: human rights, law, investigative journalism, environmental advocacy, disaster response, crisis management, and cybersecurity, among others. As OSI methods and practices are pulled in different disciplinary directions, it is important that we take stock of the overall direction and development of this highly interdisciplinary field. What new patterns of cross-collaboration are emerging? How do these diverse fields approach OSI differently in terms of methodologies, workflows, and best practices? The CEN was developed out of conversations with key actors in the field. Broadly, there was a shared sense of a lack of a collaborative, interdisciplinary space to discuss the state of the field. Ultimately, the aim within this first component is to foster such a space for dialogue, discussion, and the exchange of knowledge.

The second component aims to cultivate critical reflection on the OSI field. The objective here is to encourage OSI practitioners and researchers to critically engage with the potential ethical and epistemological limitations of current OSI methodologies and practices. How do the divisions between the embedded communities producing media evidence and those analyzing these same materials potentially weaken, ignore, or sever the possibilities for the collaborative "solidarity-based modes" of media investigation for which McAvoy advocates?

What are the power imbalances that exist in OSI workflows and methods (e.g., the dominance of an extractive relationship, where Global North groups and actors extract and take ownership of information provided by frontline global majority groups and actors)? How can the collaborative space of the CEN address these issues and help foster a more "solidarity-based" mode of OSI?

We aim to consider how we might rework and rethink OSI practices in ways that can directly respond to McAvoy's call. As she notes, we need to "integrate these digital methodologies alongside deliberate, solidarity-based practices to avoid co-opting efforts for justice or otherwise minimizing those closest to the documented harms."[9] Consequently, alongside our initial component, which engages in more practical discussions around the shape of the field and its methods and techniques of investigation, the second component aims to broaden the critical focus of our discussions, asking participants to consider how we can create more egalitarian, decolonial, and solidarity-based modes of OSI. Additionally, by engaging more effectively and systematically with affected communities, how can we shift our approaches to "justice" and "accountability" in ways that not only embrace alternative, counter-hegemonic frameworks for justice, but also help move us away from traditional Western legal and punitive frameworks of investigation? Of late, various actors and groups have been developing protocols and methodologies that can assist in making OSI-produced evidence legally admissible in human rights and criminal courts and tribunals.[10] Of course, this is important work. However, we must remain attentive to how such processes of legal translation might risk further separating content-creators from content-analyzers—leaning on Western-centric legal frameworks that might not easily map onto, or take account of, localized, community-based justice and accountability efforts.

Our first meeting was held in June 2024. It brought together a diverse range of groups and individuals in the field and assembled both practice- and research-based actors. These included individuals from the following organizations and institutions:

Bellingcat; Global Justice Investigations Lab; American University, Washington College of Law; University of Copenhagen, Views of Violence; Queen Mary University of London, School of Law; SITU Research; University College London, Urban Laboratory; Human Rights Watch; autonoma; The Sentry; Erasmus University Rotterdam, School of Law; WITNESS; University of Swansea, School of Law; Earshot; and representare. In this initial session, we discussed potential topics, themes, and problematics in the OSI field around which we could structure our discussions in future sessions. A range of shared topics and areas for exploration emerged: the ethics of OSI work (issues of consent, use of facial recognition technology, experiences of vicarious trauma); collaboration (cross-disciplinary and interdisciplinary approaches, collaboration on open data, democratization of "gate-kept" OSI technologies and tools); methodologies (AI as a tool, training around identification of synthetic data, using OSI to understand forms of structural rather than acute violence); data sharing and accessibility (sharing of data repositories, routes for advocating for governments or private companies to make more of their data open source, tracing origins of data more effectively); and legal pathways (experience and techniques for making OSI more actionable in legal processes, risks of legal adaptation and translation).

This list of potential topics, themes, and problematics is, of course, far from exhaustive. As the network builds and augments over time, we will circle back to this list to reassess and add to it. Ultimately, the CEN aims to develop an organic, collaborative, and communal space for discussion and critical reflection. OSI research can often be an isolating and fragmented experience; conducted not only at a remove from the physical sites and communities under investigation, but also often disconnected from other OSI or OSI-adjacent groups who might be able to provide fruitful critical feedback or support. As McAvoy reminds us, "collaboration is and should be the cornerstone of open source investigation." [11]

1   Miren Gutiérrez, "Democratic Practice in the Era of Platforms: From Clicktivism to Open source Intelligence," in *Democratic Institutions and Practices: A Debate on Governments, Parties, Theories and Movements in Today's World,* ed. Juan José Gómez Gutiérrez, José Abdelnour-Nocera, and Esteban Anchústegui Igartua (Cham: Springer International Publishing, 2022), 197, https://doi.org/10.1007/978-3-031-10808-2_13.

2   Yvonne McDermott, Alexa Koenig, and Daragh Murray, "Open Source Information's Blind Spot: Human and Machine Bias in International Criminal Investigations," *Journal of International Criminal Justice 19,* 1 (2021): 87, https://doi.org/10.1093/jicj/mqab006.

3   Nishat Awan, "Digital Witnessing and the Erasure of the Racialized Subject," *Journal of Visual Culture* 20, 3 (2021): 507, https://doi.org/10.1177/14704129211061182.

4   Libby McAvoy, "Centering the 'Source' in Open Source Investigation," *Open Global Rights,* January 21, 2021, https://www.openglobalrights.org/centering-the-source-in-open-source-investigation/.

5   McAvoy, "Centering the 'Source'."

6   Raja Althaibani, Libby McAvoy, and Dalila Mujagic, "Symposium on Fairness, Equality, and Diversity in Open Source Investigations: The Case To (Re)New Community of Practice for the Open Source Investigative Field," *Opinio Juris,* February 7, 2023, https://opiniojuris.org/2023/02/07/symposium-on-fairness-equality-and-diversity-in-open-source-investigations-the-case-to-renew-community-of-practice-for-the-open-source-investigative-field/.

7   McAvoy, "Centering the 'Source'."

8   McAvoy, "Centering the 'Source'."

9   McAvoy, "Centering the 'Source'."

10   See e.g. "Handbook on Civil Society Documentation of Serious Human Rights Violations," Public International Law & Policy Group, 2016; "Methodology for Online Open Source Investigations," Bellingcat and Global Legal Action Network, 2022; "Leiden Guidelines on the Use of Digitally Derived Evidence in International Criminal Courts and Tribunals," Kalshoven-Giekes Forum, 2022; "Investigative Methods: An NCRM Innovation Collection," National Centre for Research Methods, 2022; and "Outlining a Human-Rights Based Approach to Digital Open Source Investigations," The Engine Room and The Human Rights, Big Data and Technology Project, 2022.

11   McAvoy, "Centering the 'Source'."

Fortifying the Truth

Sam Gregory [SG] in Conversation with
Lisa Luksch [LL]

SAM GREGORY

Sam Gregory is an internationally recognized human rights advocate and technologist and an expert on innovations in preserving trust, authenticity, and evidence in an era of increasingly complex audiovisual communication and deception. As executive director of WITNESS, he leads their strategic plan to "Fortify the Truth" and champions their global team in support of millions of people using video and technology for human rights and civic journalism. In 2018, he established WITNESS's "Prepare, Don't Panic" initiative (gen-ai.witness.org) around deepfakes. He has testified in both the US House and Senate on AI and synthetic media and is a TED speaker on how to better prepare for the threat of deepfakes and deceptive AI.

LISA LUKSCH

Lisa Luksch is a curator at the Architecture Museum of the Technical University in Munich and a research assistant for the Chair of Architectural History and Curatorial Practice there. She studied architecture at the Technical University of Munich and the University of Antwerp and in 2023 co-curated her first exhibition, *Building to Heal: New Architecture for Hospitals.*

LISA LUKSCH Sam, you are the executive director of the human rights organization WITNESS—a group that helps people all over the world use video and technology to protect and defend their rights. Can you tell us a bit more about how WITNESS works and what defines your practice?

SAM GREGORY WITNESS is a global human rights network founded just over thirty years ago on the promise of video as a tool for sharing testimonies and showing the reality of human rights violations around the world. Over the past thirty years, we have evolved with the progression of access to a constellation of technologies. At this point, we have the technology in our mobile phones to film video as well as easy ways to edit and a variety of ways to share videos, from social media platforms to showing it directly to a decision-maker. We enable a range of people, from traditional human rights defenders to ordinary civilians, to use the tools they have—typically a mobile phone, typically access to editing—to create and share videos that are impactful on the human rights issues they care about.

The WITNESS team is globally distributed. I have colleagues in fourteen countries around the world, and we work in six regions: North America, primarily the US, Latin America and the Caribbean, Brazil, sub-Saharan Africa, the Middle East and North Africa, and South and Southeast Asia. And in each of those regions, we work with a range of human rights defenders who are also using video in a variety of ways, from community storytelling and memorialization, to legal cases, to advocating for their rights to decision-makers and the public.

We try to work at multiple levels of using video. We know that many more people have access to this incredibly persuasive tool, that it is increasingly the way people communicate: think TikTok, think YouTube Shorts, think about the ways people share videos in their family WhatsApp groups. What we do is try to make sure that the choices human rights defenders are making about how to use video are as effective, ethical, and safe as possible. What that means, practically, is that we work very closely with a network of human rights defenders on the ground to support their use of video. This includes a strong current focus around land rights issues and climate justice, particularly centering on how youth and Indigenous youth use those tools. Additionally we have a very heavy focus on how to increase the accessibility especially of Open Source Intelligence (OSINT) techniques to human rights groups on the ground working on state violence and war crimes. In those cases, my colleagues around the world are working very closely to figure out how to help existing human rights groups use these tools as part of their repertoire, their strategies. That is one layer of our work.

The second layer revolves around the question of how to make it easier for as many people as possible to tap into best practices for using video as evidence, documenting environmental crimes, or exercising their right to record. And we respond to that via a mix of digital and physical engagement. We reach over 1.5 million people a year with digital resources that are often simple videos shared on Instagram or digital tip sheets. Sometimes, people actually do meet in training sessions or receive physical documentation that helps them know how best to film, share, and use video in a way that creates an impact on the human rights issue they care about.

The third layer of our work is that we realized, close to fifteen years ago, that so much of the structure around how human rights defenders can use these technologies is established by the underlying technologies and platforms, and that you have to engage on those. Otherwise, you are disadvantaging those frontline human rights defenders. They are using tools and technologies and platforms that hinder rather than help them. That is why we work on this strategic layer, too.

Fortifying the Truth

Right now we are in a critical moment around trust and truth. We describe our work now as being about "fortifying the truth." And we describe it in those terms because it is getting harder to fight for human rights around the globe. There are more authoritarian and populist regimes. Simultaneously, the burden of proof is being escalated. So the expectations of what you show and share to prove that something happened are increasing. And then we layer on top of that the threat of AI as a challenge to our trust in what we see and hear. So we think you have to double down on how human rights defenders fortify the truth at a tactical level, at a strategy level, and at a technology and infrastructure level.

LL   Especially the third layer you described leads me to my second question: You not only work directly with individuals who want to document and expose injustice, but your efforts also tie in with technology development and policy-making. Why is this so important, and what does this cooperation look like in concrete terms?

SG   As I mentioned, about fifteen years ago we realized that the conditions set by the technologies and platforms were hindering rather than helping human rights defenders. And so we started trying to influence content moderation decisions, for example by YouTube, on whether or not to keep up a video of police violence. When we started to see that during protests in Syria, human rights defenders were trying to blur their faces in videos but did not have access to easy mobile tools, we wondered: How can we get a technology platform like YouTube to build that function in?

This built on another strand of our work that we have developed for most of the last fifteen years: In the Syrian civil war context, one of the first situations of mass human rights violations documented by civilians with their cameras, we worked with partners to start developing technologies that enabled people to more easily take a photo or video and verify the location and time and integrity of that video.

Today, we see that once again there is a discussion happening around trust in images. How do we understand where they were created, how AI was used, how humans were involved? And there, we are advocating once again on the technology infrastructure and policy, but we do it grounded in this deep understanding of how human rights defenders have these needs, but also build their own technologies and tools to respond to them.

LL   Let's get into the topic of generative AI: You have been engaging with that technology more closely since 2017, and in 2018 you launched the "Prepare, Don't Panic" program on this topic. What is it all about? And what specific recommendations do you provide?

SG   In 2017, we started to see the phenomenon of "deepfakes." At the time, there was a clear threat in the way deepfakes were being used to target primarily women with nonconsensual synthetic sexual images. And there was a rhetorical threat, where people were using this new method to create realistic-looking images of people saying something they never said, or of events that never happened, undermining our trust in real events or as part of misinformation and disinformation.

The realities that human rights defenders experienced in 2018 and since well before that are that people attack the integrity of your information, they attack you, and you are constantly fighting a battle to be heard and trusted in the public sphere. We therefore started an initiative called "Prepare, Don't Panic." The reason we called it that was the rhetorical hype around the threat of deepfakes in 2018. People were saying: "This will be the deepfake election!" or "The elections will be destroyed by the threat of deepfakes of US midterm candidates." And we already knew that the problem with that rhetoric is that it also contributes to the undermining of confidence in the people whose accounts were already dismissed, i.e., human rights defenders.

Fortifying the Truth

The "Prepare, Don't Panic" work has now been going on for more than six years. And the focus has been very much a multiple-step process. First, we repeatedly listen very closely to the expectations of the communities of human rights defenders, civic journalists, technologists, and social movement leaders in each of the regions where we work. Second, we ask them to prioritize what they need as solutions. And lastly—and this has been increasing in the last year or so—we look at how the actual usage of AI is influencing societies. We have used information from the field work we are doing and from running a rapid response mechanism for claims of suspected deepfakes as well as actual deepfakes. The Deepfakes Rapid Response Force is a global mechanism available to human rights defenders, journalists and fact checkers, bringing the examples they are confronted with to a team of forensic experts.

One task has been to argue for technological solutions grounded in the needs of a global majority and of people who are already vulnerable. We therefore do work on access to detection tools that enable people to detect synthetic content. But we do this through the lens of what we describe as "detection equity," which means that the people who actually need this the most (human rights defenders, journalists, and communities primarily in the global majority world) are the ones who are usually the least prioritized for access to the right tools, the right skills, and who are the least prioritized in terms of even the customized development of those tools. The current training sets that underlie these tools are not optimized for accented English or Burmese; they are prioritized for people who speak with US accents.

The second area of solutions drew on our work on tools for authenticity and provenance. In 2019, we published a report called "Ticks Or It Didn't Happen."[1] It summarized fourteen dilemmas you are confronted with when creating a structure for showing where media comes from, where it was created, how it was edited, and perhaps who created and edited it. And this, too, was building on our experience of creating these tools within the human rights community before it became a mainstream need. Very early on, we got involved in pushing for a human rights-based approach for building this emergent infrastructure to show how humans and AI interact in our media consumption.

LL   Can we focus once again on the second aspect you mentioned? When discussing the detection of deepfakes, data labeling is a major issue and one you already mentioned, too. How can we still ensure, for instance, that the anonymity—and I guess therefore the safety—of whistleblowers is preserved?

SG   One of the primary uniting factors in global legislation around AI is a desire to see with more clarity when AI is being used and how it is combined with human interaction. We strongly support this idea of "pipeline responsibility," reaching from the creators of foundation models to the deployers, to the tools, to us as citizens and consumers of content. It is very important to have this transparency on how AI is being used. And that is not a binary: AI or no AI. It's more like AI is part of the recipe of our everyday media consumption. And I use the word recipe because it's about how AI is used at different stages of production. You, or an AI agent, might use AI to create something. You might edit it with a human using an AI tool. You might distribute it on a platform, someone else might edit it, and that's a recipe for what we consume at the end of that process. And we need transparency to understand that process. And that, I think, is a shared part of almost every approach to legislation and norms and principles.

Drawing from our experiences and the "Ticks Or It Didn't Happen" report, we knew of the dilemmas one has to address when creating this system for tracking media production. But the underlying idea is to gain transparency on the entire process of media creation. However, critically we need to understand how this type of technical infrastructure might be misused for surveillance or to better track dissidents, whistleblowers or ordinary citizens. It's important that the question of how media is made with AI is not conflated unnecessarily with who made media at at the level of personal identity.

Recently, we have seen a profusion of fake news laws globally. Between 2016 and 2022, we had almost 100 different laws globally dealing with fake or misleading information online. A lot of the time, those laws provide a lot of discretion to governments to silence speech, target journalists and to challenge anonymity and pseudonymity. This is why we strongly believe that any kind of systematic solution needs a profound understanding of the legal frameworks that are often about suppressing speech and targeting dissent, not about reinforcing it.

LL   Finally, let's talk about precisely this point of the legislation. You presented your recommendations for dealing with AI applications to the US House Subcommittee on Cybersecurity, Information Technology, and Government Innovation in November last year. At what level do you think such regulations ought to be made and what measures are currently being taken around the world?

SG   I think there is momentum around this idea of AI transparency. It is part of the EU AI Act[2] as well as a range of international declarations such as the G7 Hiroshima AI declaration. And as you noted, it is part of a lot of discussions among national legislators. I testified to both the House side of the US Congress as well as the US Senate on this topic. I think it is important to agree on common standards, but there will always be national legislation. Obviously, a lot of rule settings will be developed by the EU and the US, but we do not yet know how, for example, the EU AI Act will play out as a rule-setting mechanism globally. I am glad to see that it actually puts a lot of emphasis on the "pipeline of responsibility" and includes elements around labeling and indicating the use of AI and the use of synthetic media and deepfakes.

The concerns I have when I think about US and EU dominance are based on a focus on their own citizens and possible ignorance toward the global implications of the decisions they make. If we are to defend questions around privacy, access, and potential weaponization that might impact the rest of the world, we need to take them into account. We also do need to be aware that there are other jurisdictions that are already making deliberately rights-compromising decisions about how to handle this. China, for example, has mandates around transparency. In some ways, they are similar to what we are seeing in other contexts, but are tied up with all the existing rules banning free speech and protecting "national security."

We are at a really interesting point, a really critical one. We have this complex picture of the actual usage of synthetic media, now that the tools are much more easily available, much more commoditized, much more commercialized. But I would argue that this year, what we need to be paying attention to is how we lay these foundations. How do we provide transparency to the public, how do we create rights-respecting ways for people to be able to understand what they're consuming? It is not going to get easier. The content will not get less photorealistic, less audio-realistic, less persuasive in 2025, 2026, 2027 . . . . The decisions we make this year about both the informal rules we set within platforms and the binding regulations set by governments and intergovernmental bodies will be decisive. It is really critical that we get it right this year! We must still prepare—and act—not panic.

---

1   "Ticks" is a British English word for checkmarks.

2   The use of artificial intelligence in the EU will be regulated by the AI Act, the world's first comprehensive AI law, published in March 2024.

Image Credits

American Colony/Matson (G. Eric and Edith) Photograph Collection, Library of Congress Prints and Photographs Division, Washington, DC: p. 111 (bottom); Ekaterina Anchevskaya: p. 91; Baidu, DigitalGlobe & spaceview: p. 85; Bellingcat, 070: p. 131 (bottom); Courtesy the Cartographic and Architectural Records at the National Archives in College Park, MD: p. 138 (top); The Center for Spatial Technologies: pp. 35 (top), 36; The Center for Spatial Technologies, derivation based on an image by Peter Andryushchenko via Telegram: p. 35 (bottom); GlobalSecurity.org: p. 77 (top left); Alison Killing and BuzzFeed News, derivation based on Google Earth Pro, 2021 CNES / Airbus: p. 86 (bottom); Robert Maher and Bellincat, 070, derivation based on Google Earth Pro, 2023 CNES / Airbus: p. 133; Abelardo Liz: p. 131 (top); LKA Bayern: pp. 117–25; Mexican General National Archive, Courtesy Centro Prodh: p. 137; New Zealand National Film Unit: p. 67 (top); Anjli Parrin: pp. 49, 52; Planet Labs PBC: pp. 63–64, 113; Jan Rothuizen: pp. 88–89; Suneil Sanzgiri: pp. 56, 67 (bottom); Courtesy SITU Research: p. 31; Courtesy SITU Research, derivation based on material provided by member attorneys from the NLG: cover and pp. 12–13, 29; Courtesy SITU Research and Centro Prodh: p. 138 (bottom); SITU Research, derivation based on NDVI data of Landsat satellite imagery, courtesy of the U.S. Geological Survey, and satellite imagery of CNES / Airbus DS: p.108 (top); SITU Research, derivation based on NDVI data of Landsat satellite imagery, courtesy of the U.S. Geological Survey, and geospatial data from OCHA: p. 107; SPOT image: pp. 74, 77 (top right, bottom); US Department of Defense: p. 73; Courtesy Yesh Din: pp. 108 (bottom), 111 (top); Alison Killing and BuzzFeed News, derivation based on YouTube, 2021 guanguan4168: p. 86 (top)

Using the QR codes in the book, you can access selected visual material to see exhibition views, updates on ongoing investigations, and even entire films. The content behind these BOOK+ QR codes will grow over time. It is not stored on web servers or in the cloud, but rather on a blockchain basis in order to forestall attacks on data and to avoid data manipulation, while guaranteeing security of access.

It's worth scanning the code from time to time for updates!

For their generous support of the exhibition we would like to thank:

Freundeskreis Architekturmuseum TUM

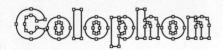

Editors:
Lisa Luksch and Andres Lepik

Project Management:
Lisa Luksch, Cristina Steingräber, and Sonja Bröderdörp

Copyediting:
Melissa M. Thorson and Dawn Michelle d'Atri

Translation:
Anna Bröderdörp

Cover Design and Design Concept:
PARAT.cc GbR, Munich

Graphic Design:
grafikanstalt, Hamburg

Reproductions:
Optische Werke, Hamburg

Printing and Binding:
Druckhaus Sportflieger, Berlin

© 2024 Architekturmuseum der Technischen Universität München (TUM), ArchiTangle GmbH, and the contributors

Architekturmuseum der TUM
at the Pinakothek der Moderne
Barer Str. 40
80333 Munich
Germany
www.architekturmuseum.de

ArchiTangle GmbH
Meierottostr. 1
10719 Berlin
Germany
www.architangle.com

ISBN 978-3-96680-032-7

All rights reserved; the contents of this publication may not be reproduced, stored in a retrieval system or transmitted without the prior written permission of the editors and the publisher.